The Last Word Is Love

My Path of Courage through War, Healing and Faith

RUTH PFAU

A Crossroad Book
The Crossroad Publishing Company
New York

The Crossroad Publishing Company
www.CrossroadPublishing.com
© 2017 by Ruth Pfau

Photographs on pages 32, 42, 49, 58, 64, 66, 71, 107, 116, 156, 164, 176 are used with permission of DAHW: The German Leprosy and Tuberculosis Relief Association, Raiffeisenstraße 3, 97080 Würzburg, Germany; www.dahw.de. Other photographs used with permission from the Marie Adelaide Leprosy Center, Mariam Manzil, A.M. 21, Off Shahrah-e-Liaquat, P.O. Box No. 8666, Saddar Karachi 74400 Pakistan; http://malc.org.pk.

Title by Ruth Pfau
Cover design by George Foster
Cover photos by Joerg-Henning Meyer
Library of Congress Cataloging-in-Publication Data available from the Library of Congress.
ISBN 978-0-8245-2369-5

Books published by The Crossroad Publishing Company may be purchased at special quantity discount rates for classes and institutional use. For information, please e-mail sales@ CrossroadPublishing.com

Contents

Part II

Preface

This book would never have been written if not for countless friends across the globe who insisted that my "Pakistan experience," this struggle of our team, should not be lost and forgotten. And if not for the friends and colleagues who put it together and made a book out of the thoughts and stories and these pieces of paper—all in German—that were lying and flying in different corners from Germany to the United States to Pakistan.

And if not for my successors, my management team, who took over for me when I was sixty-five and was putting my house in order, who insisted in writing down—in English—this story to which so many have contributed, investing their lives, risking their lives, *living* their lives for the cause.

This is my story, the story of a German who has by now lived more than forty years in Pakistan, and has been very happy in her work, and with her patients, friends, and co-workers; who loves the laughter and the sadness and the courage of the people, the beauty and the threatening grandeur of the country; who has suffered a lot witnessing the injustice and the violence and disregard for the dignity of the weak and the poor; and who has tried and struggled to add her small contribution to the fight against evil and strengthen the many, many good and brave initiatives.

But, of course, I have seen it with the eyes of a Westerner. And as this book is a kind of account of my life, there will be many passages strange to my Muslim friends. But this may not necessarily be a negative point because this mutual intercultural enrichment, which characterizes the leprosy program of Pakistan, has only been possible because we have *shared*, listened, and clarified our ways of thinking, making this cross-fertilization possible.

Part 1 is the account of the beginning of this totally crazy, irrational adventure, which seems even to me today, when I look back, so utterly unbelievable. This adventure, which in the beginning was defined as "we first control leprosy in Karachi, then in Pakistan, then we'll go to China, and then to the moon!"

Part 2 is written after a long life. It surely still has enough of the original adventurous flavor but as it unfolds it is different. The world has changed, Pakistan has changed, and surely my outlook has changed as well. Life has disillusioned me, and this is an advantage. I have less illusion and therefore hope that today I am closer to truth than I was in the prime of the beginning.

Truth is often painful. You need courage, *you do need courage* not to look aside when truth, *truth,* reveals itself as hurtful. That the team kept the original ideals, the dream, the "c. i." (corporate identity), this is one of the precious gifts in my life. We have gone through the fallout of the September 11 catastrophe, the Afghanistan war, the Iraq war, and

A familiar scene in the many years of Ruth Pfau's work: a member of a large family is suffering from a serious illness, in most cases probably leprosy or tuberculosis. After treatment, and sometimes contrary to expectations, the patient is healthy again. And after years it comes again and again—encounters full of gratitude and joy. Photo: Bernd Hartung

all that has and is happening afterward and, in all the uncertainty the second millennium has brought us, the team, after having controlled leprosy, has embarked on rendering the same services to Pakistan in the field of tuberculosis and blindness control, and to disabled patients who have been utterly neglected in Pakistan.

Thus, this account is also an expression of the hope that our story may help increase the Pakistani *ownership* of the program; that after Germany has owned the work and paid the bills for forty years, the citizens of Pakistan will now provide the support and resources to the dedicated and competent new leadership team so that it can extend its services further.

There is still so much to do, so much misery in the country! I hope and pray that in the next forty years we are instrumental in rehabilitating our leprosy patients and giving them back their dignity; lessening the suffering of tuberculosis patients and restoring them to health and happiness; preventing patients from turning unnecessarily blind; and giving hope and dignity to disabled patients.

And so I dream that this book will give a bit of hope to those who succumb to the all-pervading discouragement that "good" has only a very small chance in life, and that peace, including peace among different religions and cultures, is impossible. This is not true. The conclusion of my long life—in spite of all the shed and unshed tears it has cost me—is that it has been worthwhile. That it is worthwhile. It is worthwhile.

Ruth Pfau
Karachi

PART 1

1
Homeward Bound
1984

I often ask myself when returning to Pakistan what this country actually means to me. A clearly defined answer does not easily come to mind, just as life itself, with all its fathomless human secrets, cannot be clearly defined.

But one thing is certain to me: coming back to Pakistan is a return to a place where I actually belong. I have never doubted my life decisions—joining the order and with it the renunciation of married life, a career, and further studies, and the decision to come to Karachi. In this respect my life is firmly anchored and secure. I believe, or rather *I know*, that I am in the place where the *Almighty* wants me to be.

> I believe, or rather *I know*, that I am in the place where the *Almighty* wants me to be.

Another thing is also certain: I love the people of this country, those with whom I work, my team, my boys, and all those who have devoted their lives to leprosy work. And I love my patients—they need me and I need them.

Each time when I get off the plane (mostly still wrapped up in winter woollies) I am overcome by the sticky heat and tropical climate of Karachi: 40 degrees Celsius (104 degrees Fahrenheit) and 80 percent atmospheric humidity. There is an indescribable confusion at the airport, a festive atmosphere full of heat and noise, the clamor of noisy conversations, the persistence of porters and taxi drivers and all those trying to attach themselves to new arrivals in the hope of earning something. When I finally emerge from this noisy, swirling sea of life I know that I am … at home? No, not at home, but where I *want* to be.

Then it all starts again, the burning compassion and the nagging guilty conscience. If I *were not* picked up in triumph by members of my congregation, a minibus full of Punjabi girls who snatch up my luggage, then the boy who tries so hard to offer his services as a porter would be proud to take home a well-earned ten rupees and the taxi driver would also earn his share. And so on.

This pulsating, colorful turmoil, the shimmering sun, the heat, the dust, the ceaseless honking of car horns in traffic that can only be described as chaotic—speeding rickshaws weaving in and out of a mess of heavily laden trucks, gaudily painted buses with passengers packed in like sardines, an occasional decorated camel laden with bundles of cotton—all this has by now become a part of me.

Pakistan, this country of mine, a land of contrasts: the seemingly never-ending expanse of Balochistan, where an encounter with a lonely shepherd is an event, where the camel rider on the horizon seems like a mirage on the edge of an endless nothingness.

And the glacier, glistening in its silent inaccessible majesty; the Himalayas by moonlight; the mothers who have learned to live with life's pain, silently and without complaint; the children, whose only playground is the mud and slime of some illegal hutment; and our patients—Paul, with his stumps for arms, creating riotously colored flowers on paper with a felt pen, and Ahmed, limping every morning to work on his deformed feet. All this is to be found here.

Yes, I love Pakistan. I love it with every beat of my heart, with helpless pain and surging anger when I see the social injustice and the lack of concern.

When all is said and done, I am a foreigner and will remain one. Still, returning is a kind of homecoming for me, because this country, after so many long years, has become my home.

2

The Encounter

Being an Onlooker Is Difficult

I had not planned on actually coming to Pakistan. I belong to a religious order. My superiors had asked me to go to India and I agreed. But the visa was a long time in coming. I waited for almost eighteen months. Just at that time Pakistan was looking for a lady doctor. Perhaps my dreamed-of goal could be reached there. I seized the chance and took off.

That I had wanted to go abroad at all had a lot to do with the situation in Germany at the time. The "Economic Miracle" was in the making, but it had not yet pervaded all aspects of life. This level of affluence was new to me. In those days Misereor, an international development agency of the Catholic Church in Germany, was distributing the first information on the developing world. I saw how inequality flourished. It horrified me that there were people for whom hunger, cold nights, and homelessness were permanent facts of life, unlike the Germans for whom the postwar period was just a terrible passing phase. If I could not change everything I at least wanted to share this suffering. Doing nothing seemed intolerable.

There is a book titled *Gehenna* that I read as a child. I do not even remember who the author is. As a twelve-year-old the contents were unintelligible to me. My parents had even forbidden me to read it. The last chapter, however, made a deep impression on my mind. It was about a prison camp. One of the warders could not bear to witness the suffering of the prisoners any longer so one day he simply disappeared. Months later his friend was ordered to carry out a dying person. Shocked, he recognized his friend in the starved heap of bones. The last words of the man left a deep imprint in my heart: "It is much more difficult to stand by and look on than to be there and suffer together."

Opel or Volkswagen?

I could not understand the preoccupation of the Germans of those days. It was a time when one felt that one should amass everything that one wanted. It was a period of gluttony in which one tended to stuff oneself with everything that was previously unobtainable. I surely understood a certain "catching up," but not to this extent. When someone snatches a sweet from a child's mouth the child will naturally start whining and try to get another. But when someone gobbles up too many sweets he will simply ruin his stomach. I was at a loss to understand what amusement there could possibly be in feeling bloated.

Looking back, I remember one day we were sitting in the doctors' mess. I had just earned my driving license. We were discussing among ourselves which kind of car would be the best to buy. The Volkswagen (in Germany, we nickname them "Beetles")? Should it be an orange or dove gray one? Or maybe an Opel would be even better! Suddenly, I thought, was *this* the only meaning of life—saving money, buying cars, saving more money, changing cars? That evening I called on the provincial superior of my religious order. I wanted to get out. Soon, and if possible, immediately. To Asia, where one lived on just a handful of rice per day.

A Dropout for the Sake of the Poor

Finally, after a long and exhausting wait, I was on my way—fleeing from an array of consumer goods that bored me, fleeing from all this meaningless materialism that had become unbearable for me. I was on my way to Pakistan.

I will never forget my arrival in Karachi. It was my very first flight and I left Paris on a clear blue March morning with a blissfully adventurous feeling. There was a stopover in Rome. The laurel trees were in blossom and the first spring roses had made their appearance. I reveled in the gold and splendor, in the austere beauty of ancient Rome.

Then came the final departure from Europe. I had gone away with the firm decision never to return, to become an Asian, a dropout for the sake of the poor. How disappointed I was when dinner was served on the plane, such a sumptuous menu with so many exotic courses!

After a rather bumpy flight we landed in Tehran. Between Tehran and Karachi there was only the desert, spread out like some giant sheet—gray, unreal, fantastic. Shadows and grain looked like a marble floor in St. Peter's Basilica in Rome. Occasionally an oasis—not like the oases of my childhood dreams—a lonely mud hut under a clump of dusty date palms; otherwise, just wasteland, solitude, oblivion. The long-awaited announcement, after hours of wasteland far below, "In a few minutes we shall be landing in Karachi." Beneath stood a few barracks in the desert sand, some bare and desolate hills, and the sea on the horizon. All this came as a sudden shock. I thought that I must have been in a state of mental derangement to have allowed myself to be carted off to these sands of desolation. It was March and as I disembarked, wrapped in a winter coat, I found it unbearably hot. I had been rather airsick and had not eaten much on the flight.

> It is much more difficult to stand by and look
> on than to be there and suffer together.

The room to which they brought me had only a half partition dividing it from the next. On the other side some girls had a radio blaring so loudly that I picked up my suitcase and moved out. I was completely and utterly exhausted and my blood sugar was by now very low. I definitely thought that a young person like myself, in a foreign land, should not have been received so casually. I decided not to stay.

The Morning That Decided Everything

My first subjective impressions of community life in Karachi: in the morning, classes; in the afternoon, washing and ironing clothes. It took me at least three weeks before I could make myself understood in English. Then Berenice Vargas, a Mexican sister who was a qualified pharmacist, took me to the slums. We at once became friends. In the mornings Berenice supervised a kindergarten run by the order. In the afternoons she went to the leprosy colony. One afternoon I decided to accompany her. It was the day that decided everything, that was to change everything in my life. The McLeod Road Leper Colony, to which she took me after a few weeks of comparative comfort in the community house,

Sister Berenice Vargas (center) and "Mother" Françoise Fabrte (right) visit the site of their future work on the McLeod Road. The hut was later bought for 300 rupees (about 40 euros).

was an illegal settlement of slum hovels. One of Karachi's most notorious districts, it was situated near the main railway station, beside the busy commercial and banking heart of Pakistan. Here were the poorest of the poor, beggars suffering from leprosy, simply vegetating in huts made of cardboard boxes and bamboo sticks, covered with rotting gunny bags, some just a pair of ragged straw mats joined together, none of them waterproof. And in the midst of everything, this misery, this lamentable and hopeless misery: deformed anaesthetic hands and feet, prey for the rats at night; filth and vermin; drugs and brawls. About one hundred and fifty leprosy patients lived here in indescribable filth. Unimaginable, yet real, even by Karachi standards at the time. A colony in the middle of the city, in a kind of hollow, which during the rainy season became actually knee-deep in filthy drainage water, a stinking lake of horror and misery. And yet drinking water had to be brought and carried into the huts.

Today it all sounds like some cheap, sensational story in the popular press. But in those days it was the truth—the touchable, smellable, feelable, and hearable truth.

When One Meets One's Greatest Love

The Marie Adelaide Leprosy Dispensary was initiated here by France de Chevillotte, a French social worker and member of our order. Hence the name, after Marie Adelaide de Cicé, who founded the Society of the Daughters of the Heart of Mary in the midst of revolutionary turmoil in Paris in the 1790s.

Leprosy patients from all parts of the city and country came for help and treatment. And this was the dispensary, the outpatient department made of old packing cases, with only two tiny windows and without water or electricity. The room was crammed with patients. Added to this was the unbearable heat inside this box, the evil stench, and the noise. Asia can be such an ear-splitting noisy continent and here was no exception. And the flies … the flies formed a buzzing pall over everything.

But the thing that shocked me most was a patient, about my age, nearly thirty, a certain Muhammad Rashid. He came from the mountains in the north of the country, and he crawled on his hands and feet like a dog, on all fours. His fellow patients walked calmly around him, unperturbed, as if it was all very normal that a human being had to crawl in such a manner in the dirt and slime. It would not perhaps have been quite so shocking if Muhammad Rashid had not taken it so calmly. There was just dull resignation in his eyes, as if things could not have been otherwise. And he, too, had only one life to live, one single life, a life just like mine!

This consent to degradation stunned me. That these people took their condition to be normal, that they had become resigned to such frightfulness, was for me the limit in human degradation. If they could have shown that they were suffering I would have been able to communicate with them somehow. In the postwar years in Germany we used to say: "It can't go on like this anymore. We must—*we must*—work for change." Here, nobody thought of saying anything like that. I very rarely have attacks of sudden rage, moments in which I am no longer in control of myself, yet suddenly I knew something had to happen here. But how? Something had to be done on the spot. "Berenice," I said with suppressed emotion, "Berenice, it can't go on like this anymore. We'll do something. Here and now, we do something, positively, anything, but we won't watch any longer!" My heart was pounding. It was like meeting one's great love. This was now decided, and this was forever. Everything else was only the outcome of that moment in the beggar colony on McLeod Road.

It can't go on like this anymore.
We must—*we must*—work for change.

Berenice sighed a sigh of relief: "I expected it," she said, "the way you have been described to me when they announced you."

Two people's destiny had met.

Operation in the Mortuary

There must have been no second place in Pakistan where misery was so accentuated as in this leper colony. I believe that anyone who has a medical degree like me would have acted in the same way. One just cannot stand by when people like us, who have the same right to dignity and happiness, are allowed to rot in filth and disease, worse than dogs in the street. I was not left with any other choice. Perhaps it was my experience with the Jews during Germany's Third Reich that aroused in me this passionate longing for justice. Nothing could have prevented me from helping them, not even the mistrust of the patients themselves or scorn of my colleagues in the medical world. I would not have cared if my motives were called into question, if I were accused of merely wanting to convert the patients to Christianity. I found myself in the midst of suffering fellow humans who needed help. There was simply no other alternative but to go ahead.

I still remember vividly the death of one of my first patients, due to a kidney complication caused by untreated leprosy. We did not live in the colony but we came every day. I was concerned about the reaction of the other patients, how they would cope with his death. With our meager resources I did not hold out much hope. The laboratory tests that were available showed a similar hopelessness. When my patient finally died I was in tears. But his fellow patients said, "Nobody ever before had died as beautifully as Salman." It deeply consoled me that it was seen as a service when somebody could die with dignity. I was determined that we would continue.

At that time operations were carried out in the huts themselves, kneeling on the dirt floors. A patient would sit by my side, keeping the flies at bay with a bamboo fan. Here I was, a graduate from one of the newly built, modern hospitals of West Germany. I could never have believed that the same service performed in a sterile polyclinic, helping people in need, could be carried out on almost every street corner of this teeming two-million-person city, too.

Soon after we had to operate on an emergency case among our patients in the mortuary of a government hospital. It was a question of life and death; we could not delay any longer. We were not able to even get a garage in the city where we could bring our leprosy patients. "I'd just love to help you, but you must realize that I couldn't put my reputation at stake by letting in leprosy patients." This was the excuse so often presented to me. We were able to get into the mortuary because, by this time, I had gotten to know someone involved in the hospital management.

Through the years I have learned that one can wrangle something out even of the most impossible situations, but only if one is stubborn and not put off by setbacks. Although our little dispensary was only made of packing cases and had no electricity or running water, we were able to carry on professionally sound rather than dabbling in quackery or lowering standards. Laboratory examinations and x-rays were available and I was in touch with specialist clinics. Bandages were made from clean bedsheets and neatly rolled, and soon medical supplies were donated from countries abroad—anti-leprosy drugs, antibiotics, cortisone, vitamin tablets and drips for the howling, skinny babies.

With the aid of bamboo sticks and old sacks sewn together, we erected a sun shelter in front of the dispensary. By 1962 there were over nine hundred patients but the dispensary was still the same eight-by-eight meters. In one corner, medicines were handed out, and in another corner Abdul Rehman had set up his laboratory. Another corner served as a physiotherapy department, complete with wax bath and massage facilities. The remaining space was taken by the dressing department.

The year 1961 was a time of an exceptionally heavy monsoon. For generations Karachi had not seen such a downpour. Hardly a drop had fallen in five years, just brief showers. In 1961, however, we were able to see the monsoon in its full fury. It rained so heavily that in the house where I lived every available helper was busy sweeping the water out of the rooms. It flowed like a waterfall from the roof, cascaded down the stairs, and flooded everything. But in our leprosy colony! The water was more than knee-deep—and such filthy water at that, mixed with all the rubbish and drainage from the city. The canal system is by no means suitable when it rains, and after any heavy downpour the canals and gutters overflow. In the dispensary we had to stand on tables or else wade knee-deep in a slimy, soupy mess. Fortunately we were wearing rubber boots. Previously we had gone barefoot on such occasions but with so much dirty water there was a danger of infection. The patients, with their pus-filled wounds, had to wade through this stinking lake the whole day. As I arrived in the colony, with my dress pulled up over my knees, I was unceremoniously deposited on a shabby old bicycle and pushed through the murky water to the dispensary. I still had some calls to make. The bicycle seemed somewhat risky so I was offered a rattling wooden handcart used by a crippled patient when he went begging. I was pushed along in this through the colony.

We had already been fighting for eight months to get a place to build a hospital. Our patients were still living in the sewer waters of the city.

When Miracles Occur

The miracle was definitely the response to our prayers. Actually there really were two miracles. The first one: Dr. Zarina Fazelbhoy. This upper-class lady, tall and outstandingly good-looking, who one day appeared wrapped in a silk sari in front of our dispensary, this shabby wooden hut in the leprosy ghetto. She introduced herself. She was a dermatologist. She wanted to help and wondered whether there was anything she could do. (Was there anything she could do!)

I no longer remember how I kept her occupied. But I remember vividly what I thought on this day—that she should not take my precious time to show off. That society lady who would brag about her adventures among the "outcasts" once she was sitting with her clan and her friends (all upper-class ladies), sipping tea and gossiping. I was pretty sure she would never come back. But Zarina did come. Again. And again. And in the course of time she became my closest friend and an indispensable and strong supporter of the cause.

After all, people could somehow understand that nuns like Berenice and me would do such foolish things. They soon started admiring us, reluctantly, but none of them felt obliged to imitate these foreign nuns! But when Zarina—known in the circles of the "upper two thousand" to whom she belonged—joined, when soon her son and daughter joined the team, the matter looked different. In all those long years until her untimely death in 1999, she was a staunch supporter of the work,

The step from the improvised dispensary to organized hospital was complete, made possible with the financial support of Misereor and German Leprosy Relief Organization, and with the help of the local doctor, Dr. Zarina Fazelbhoy, a loyal companion from the very beginning. The new name: Marie Adelaide Leprosy Center (MALC).

professionally but more so in the field of public awareness, soliciting funds, taking up for disowned and rejected leprosy patients, getting the government involved, using her charm and influence to gradually gain a place for the program in the hearts and minds of the Pakistani people.

In 1963, the second miracle occurred. Up to 1962, most of the nine hundred patients registered used to come to our consultation hours in the dispensary shed. Had someone told me earlier that I would treat twenty-five hundred patients a month, with no form of health insurance, I would have laughed him out of town. We were working twelve hours a day in the treatment room and still had the feeling that half the work remained unfinished. By the end of the year the monthly consultations had increased to forty-five hundred. Some of my medical colleagues asked me why I had taken up the dirtiest and most difficult work in Karachi. Even after explaining the need to work in neglected areas they remained unconvinced.

I was never a woman for big projects. Originally, I used to think along more intellectual lines rather than this struggle against naked misery, hunger, filth, rats, and flies; against drugs, smuggling, and prostitution. Yet somehow there *was* something if not intellectual then so highly spiritual in this open assault on injustice. As the misery flowed over me like a tidal wave, I began to understand some Urdu and comprehend what was going on. Grisly stories, frightful reality, a life so crude and cruel that I could never have thought of anything like that existing. I felt there were only two possibilities: go home by the quickest route or get out of the boat and walk on the water. I chose the latter. Today I know that this was the only logical answer. The beginning of the answer to the question which had haunted me after the war: how one could break out of the senselessness of an overhanging destiny.

> That this face would become beautiful as
> soon as someone began to love it.
> With this song in my heart, I started afresh.

In March 1963, the miracle, which no one dared to expect and yet which in our deepest hearts we *knew* would one day occur, actually happened. We obtained a modern hospital in the very heart of the city. In the wake of this miracle came new friends and colleagues, government recognition for our training school, an operating theater, spacious wards, specialists, three outpatient clinics in the suburbs of Karachi, twenty-four hundred registered patients and nine newly opened outclinics in every part of West Pakistan from the Himalayas to the Arabian Sea. All this happened by 1966. Yet only four years before we could not have imagined all this in our wildest dreams, certainly not when I was kneeling on the floor of a pitiful hut, operating on a patient, another patient beside me fanning away the flies. I never imagined that I would be able to do rounds again, dressed in a clean white doctor's coat, to discuss cases with a colleague, or turn on a tap over a washbasin and have the luxury of soap and towels.

The acquisition of this centrally located hospital is a story in itself. The owner had offered it to the leprosy project and it was paid for in hard currency from Germany. Misereor, an international development agency of the Catholic Church in Germany, paid for it. A friend told me at the time that, according to Pakistani law, it was very difficult to evict anyone once they were in possession of property but that it was very easy to prevent one from taking possession. Because the neighbors were bound to protest a leprosy hospital on their doorstep, we moved in stealthily at night. Our meager furniture was loaded onto donkey carts and our first two patients were admitted. The following morning at 8 a.m. we attended to three outpatients.

As far as the law was concerned we were an established hospital. In the beginning we did not dare to install windowpanes. Everything from stones to rotten eggs and tomatoes was hurled through the windows. There were also lengthy court cases from our opponents. Famous leprologists and international organizations rallied at our side with documents. For each instance, after a face-saving period, the matter was quietly dropped.

Right up to the present we have resisted all temptations to move to the city outskirts. Our place is where the people are. On this tiny piece of land in the heart of downtown Karachi a modern eight-story building has risen, the Marie Adelaide Leprosy Center. This is the miracle that happens when one meets one's greatest love.

With a Song in My Heart

I could write about my life today in one way and the next day I could write a totally different version. There is no fully completed picture. Sometimes memories become cloudy. Perhaps this is because I have lived through whole periods with my eyes closed. Certainly I have managed to achieve a lot. But I am no "doer" type. The basis of my philosophy is instrumentalism, abandonment to God's providence.

There were times when I felt the urge to reach for the stars and moments when I only could see the stars mirrored in the puddles by the roadside. In 1962 I returned from a refresher course in gloriously lush southern India and was immediately confronted with the misery of the colony. I could only see the shacks. I could only hear the noise. I could only smell the stench. The colony had become more vulgar and uglier than before. The thought that I would not be able to love it as I had before made me panic. But the words of a song by the French Jesuit Aimé Duval came back to me: "That ugly face which has never known a kiss …" That this face would become beautiful as soon as someone began to love it. With this song in my heart, I started afresh.

There were days when I could not work out whether the phrase "God so loved the world" was a blasphemy or a prayer. There were the perennial ups and downs, the ebb days. But now I can see that whenever one has left the tunnel, the darkness can be forgotten. After the birth of a child a mother no longer remembers the pain.

3

The Long Road

Early Childhood

When the Nazis came to power I was four years old. When war broke out I was ten. In spite of all this I experienced a sheltered childhood, at least until I was a little older. We were five girls and I was number four. The sixth child was a boy. When I was born, a tiny twenty-five hundred grams (about 5½ pounds), my mother said that when all the others had gone away and married, Ruth would stay behind. But I also was to go away.

I grew up with the feeling of being rather special. I was about eight or nine when my father took me to the office of the publishing firm where he was a commercial manager. "This is my *daughter!*" was how he presented me to his colleagues. As I descended the huge staircase at the end of the visit I had an unforgettable feeling of uniqueness.

Then there is the story of the red card. We Pfau children grew up with the childhood fantasy that we had some secret authorization to do things that were forbidden for "normal" people. This authorization supposedly went back to the time of one of our imaginary ancestors who possessed a certain red card. Whoever was in possession of such a card could play on grass that was forbidden to set foot on or ride a bicycle along private roads. If a custodian of the law happened to appear, one could nonchalantly produce the magic red card and the poor policemen would almost collapse, give a ceremonious salute, and then beat a very hasty retreat. That was in my early childhood, and there never was, of course, any such red card. But that rebelliousness against orders remains with me even today. An example is Azad Kashmir. I would not have established a leprosy control program there so speedily if it had not been a forbidden area for foreigners. Once as I was standing near the border I was told that Muzaffarabad was "just over there" but it was out of bounds because I was not a Pakistani. At that moment, I swore that

I would rather die than not see Muzaffarabad and the valleys of Azad Kashmir. Today Muzaffarabad is my second home and Azad Kashmir is my most successful leprosy and even tuberculosis control program.

The War Years

My childhood was not without its traumas. Today, whenever I come across mass demonstrations or riots I start to panic and have to stop and pull myself together. There are sinister memories of military parades in the park opposite our house and the noise of drums during Nazi festivals.

My father did not seem to conform to any clichés. He was an honest yet successful businessman. By today's standards he was a "green alternative," a pillar of society. He was deeply disturbed by the mass murder of Jews and considered joining the underground resistance. My mother used to argue, "When you have brought six children into the world you must understand that you are also there for their sake." This conflict was never aired in front of us children; it just smouldered. One time, when my eldest sister was at home on holiday from service, she made some remark that referenced concentration camps. My mother immediately cut her short. I remembered too that there was a Jewish girl at school who disappeared after the infamous Kristallnacht of the Nazis. It made me very nervous. I received no answer to my question, "Where has Gabi gone?"

During my school days I despised the primitive nature of the Nazis. The emphasis was on sport and a kind of "biceps culture" was fostered. Our leader in the youth group used to give me almost special treatment and this suited me as I was used to playing first fiddle. One day, our class was discussing the philosopher Nietzsche. Suddenly came the sentence, "The greatest bravery is to look on unconcerned when someone is suffering." This was too much for me to accept. I ran out of the class, pursued by my group leader. She wanted to explain what it meant, to soften it a bit for me. "No!" I shouted and I ran home and wept uncontrollably.

World War II came. In later years I was to go through two wars in Pakistan. When I heard the air-raid sirens in Karachi it brought back memories of those nightmarish air raids during the war years in Germany. In 1943 we were bombed out. There was this feeling of utter insecurity—life could not be trusted. It was proven, again and again, by the daily horrors witnessed: images of the wounded, people soaked in blood, houses bombed to pieces and ruins everywhere, all where once a securely built world had so neatly stood. Year after year I lived with a subconscious panic. The nightly blackouts and the subsequent air raids gave me a fear of the dark, which lingered on for years afterward. Even now, the same fear of darkness haunts me. Only if a patient were in danger of his life would I venture out in the dark alone. But for us children there was also a whiff of adventure, a delight in heroism. The Nazis were able to put this to use. We children used to run messages over territory covered with unexploded mines and distribute food in the emergency shelters. I did not mind distributing food—at least it helped some of the innocent victims of this evil war. But searching for adventure was only an effort to cope with the terrible truth and the deeply rooted fears; at that time the overriding fear was for my mother, who was soon to give birth to a baby.

Leipzig is roughly in the center of Germany and streams of refugees came there from all over the country in the spring of 1945. We girls were serving in civilian volunteer corps in the disaster areas, carrying boxes of supplies and handing out food. I can still see a little boy, about age four. I found him alone and crying at the railway station. He could not tell me his name; he was too afraid. I did not quite know what to do. I made an announcement over the loudspeaker that I had found a boy about four years old, and anyone who had lost him should … etc. A frightful situation. Trains were pulling out with people still trying to clamber inside. One could almost recognize the refugees from bombed-out Dresden by their horrified expressions. They had emerged from a holocaust. And here I was with this youngster, and I did not know what to do. Suddenly a woman ran up to me, ripped the child from my arms, and disappeared into the milling crowd. She must have been his mother.

There was panic and a feeling of utter helplessness. For fourteen hours a day we dragged luggage from one platform to another to help people move somehow further on. But where could they go? The whole area was surrounded by allied forces and there were constant air raids. We were only young girls and hardly knew what we were doing. We only knew that we could not just stand around.

It was amazing that, at the end of all those dark times full of horror, there should have been something strangely comforting. "Victory or defeat!" We had all been living on this slogan. Since we all knew that victory could not be won, we had made ourselves ready for a dignified defeat. At that time there was a much-read story from Roman times in circulation. A certain tribe refused to accept submission and all threw themselves voluntarily into the smouldering crater of Mount Vesuvius. This story gave wings to heroic children's dreams. When our destruction did not, in fact, take place, we were rather surprised.

We had a green garden gate. I sat on it and hummed a tune. It was a day in May; the cherry trees were in blossom and the war had come to an end. The Americans had just marched in the day before and their planes were flying above us. But we knew that they would not be bombing us this time; in any case, they had already occupied the city. And I thought, "I didn't think I'd survive this nightmare, this destruction, but life goes on." Spring flowers were beginning to peep through the rubble opposite our house. For me, that has become a living experience—that life goes on. Winter had begun to furl its somber cloak and somewhere a blackbird was singing.

What came after is full of the deepest horrors. The Americans had handed the city over to the Russians. My father had not yet returned home and my mother lay dangerously ill. We five girls were in danger of being raped by Russian soldiers in revenge for the raping, looting, and pillaging conducted by German soldiers during their military successes in the Soviet Union from 1941 to 1943.

There was also anxiety for our daily bread. The supply system had totally broken down. The baby was only one year old and my mother was very sick and unable to breastfeed him. Before sunrise my father and I would sneak through the Russian lines to look for something to bring home, but the little boy became weaker day by day.

In spite of the nightly curfew my father went out one night to get the doctor. She could not come, however, because of the curfew. I nearly went out of my mind when the child died in the night. I had always had so much love for him, even before he was born. How we used to run here and there to find milk for him! I hardly dare think of it even now. It was during this period that I sometimes thought parents ought not to bring children into the world.

Because my mother was very sick I had taken time off school so that I could manage the household. There was no coal to be had and the winter had arrived with vengeance. When we could not find anything to use as firewood we were sometimes able to steal it. We all lived in one small room so that we could take advantage of the only heater in the house in use at the time; finding enough firewood to heat the other rooms was unthinkable. It was our dining room and workroom, and it was in this room that I prepared myself for the equivalent to the Higher Cambridge examination. When I went to bed my breath froze onto my quilt. I used to get up at 3 a.m. so that I could study without disturbance, when everyone else was sleeping. They were not exactly idyllic times.

The Long Road to Inner Peace

I had no ideology then, no system of values, but I was searching for something. There was always the possibility of communism. All my former friends from Hitler's National Socialist Girls' Federation reemerged under the flag of the Young Communist League. I saw the same thing over and over again but under different colors, and could not bring myself to join in. For me the meaning of death and love was the important thing and I saw that both systems could offer nothing regarding this question.

I used to admire an assistant medical director when I was a trainee. She used to tell me that Marxism was a dynamic philosophy because it was based on scientific facts. I put the question concerning love to her but she did not answer. Then one evening I asked her if she would object to me going over to the West if the chance ever arose. "Don't worry, go if you like. I know that you'll come back. You'll soon see that Marxism is the only true way."

Shortly after the currency reform in 1948 I went over to the West. There did not seem to be any prospects for progress and I felt that I could not continue any more under such a system. The educational curriculum had become contaminated with atheistic ideology. Also important, my father could not find a job. His publishing firm had been nationalized. Moreover, his colleagues and business contacts were all in the West.

I crossed over the border illegally, not even knowing where exactly it was. It was night. A young communist boarder guard, with whom I had discussed philosophy as I dodged between trains, asked me, "Do you think you're making a right decision in going off to the West?" He himself seemed to be in doubt, but he pointed out the train to the terminal. Then I had to ask where the border was. Nobody wanted to answer. They all seemed afraid, too afraid to talk. I remember very clearly a man who had just finished shaving—he still had shaving cream on his chin. Almost in tears I said, "I must get across the border. Where do I find it?" Without speaking he gave a nod in the general direction. I walked for miles along mountain slopes, and then beneath me I saw a clearing. To hide myself I sneaked into a barn. Then three border guards, young chaps, came from the clearing. They searched my bag (I only had a briefcase with me). On top was my teddy bear, my companion since childhood, and below a few personal bits and pieces. There simply was not time to pack more. One of them said, "I'll have to take you to the camp." Together we marched over some more slopes to a nearby wood. Suddenly he said, "About two hundred meters farther on you'll find the border and there you can cross into the West. I will watch from here."

A prohibited demarcation zone lay in front of me but I just ran, my heart pounding. When I reached the Western part, exhausted, sweaty, and out of breath, I looked back. The young border guard was standing at the edge of the woods. I waved. He waved back.

Then I went on, farther into the unknown. I had just passed under a bridge when I almost collided with a soldier. A solitary soldier in this deserted no man's land. I kept on walking along the narrow path until I had passed him. After a few seconds I looked back. I seemed so utterly unbelievable that the young chap in uniform had not taken advantage of the situation. And I thought, "So this is the difference—I am in the West."

The reunion with my father was simply wonderful. But a difficult period was soon to follow. We had to bring my mother and little sister across the border and this was no easy task. We had to pay agents who specialized in bringing people across the border illegally. In the meantime, we had tried to telephone my mother in Leipzig. Just as we got connected the line was cut. I could imagine what she must have gone through during those moments. After three hefty payments we managed to get them over to the West.

We were all reunited. But it was still a difficult time for us. We lived in one rented room in Wiesbaden. When I wanted to take a bath my father had to go for a walk. My father had started up again in publishing. He was somewhat sad that none of the children had chosen the same profession, although for a short time I became his assistant. I was unable to fit permanently into the business world, however, and decided to renew my studies.

I was determined to study medicine. During the time prior to my university admission I made a bicycle tour of the Rhine Valley. Alone I cycled to Maria Laach Abbey, a famous old Benedictine monastery set in picturesque surroundings. I did not know much about religion at the time and I was unaware that monks differed from those in the Middle Ages I had read about in novels. I had even thought that Maria Laach was an art museum and I was surprised to find that the monks I saw were real and not stuffed.

> It seemed as if God had already planned something for my life, something that the monks in their black habits and the teenager in her summer outfit were at that time blissfully unaware of.

The monastery stable boy was a friendly lad. He packed my knapsack full of pears from the cloister garden and told me stories about the abbot, who had always wanted to study music but was sent off to Rome to study canon law. And he went, although he was not—positively was not—at all interested in law. I asked him if it was permitted to go into the church. "Permitted? What a funny question. Of course it is," he said. And even if I were not a Catholic? I told him that I had not even been baptized. (In the sect to which my parents belonged there was only adult baptism.)

On the eventful summer's day in 1950, it seemed as if God had already planned something for my life, something that the monks in their black habits and the teenager in her summer outfit were at that time blissfully unaware of. Two important events of my life occurred on this day. I had my first encounter with the church and I fell in love for the first time, with a traveling companion I had met on the way.

The young lad with whom I struck up a friendship came out of a Nazi stronghold. It was amazing how he managed to emerge intact from those gruesome times. However, we soon had to separate as both of us were going to study. We made a vow to write on a certain day after seven years; that is, if we were not already married. He was going to send me seven yellow roses, and I promised to reply. I got the roses. But it was not destined to be a lifelong commitment.

Finally, I began my studies. Probably everybody tends to idealize their college days but really it was a period of awakening, of starting anew. Basic questions took the air, became imprinted in our lives. We had the same determined feeling as many of those who returned from the front: Never again war! Never again fascism! Never again persecution of Jews!

"Never again" was a completely spontaneous impulse. It was a time of boundless searching. I attended left wing election meetings and was fascinated by the open and frank expression of opinion. I joined the Socialist Students Union and got myself elected as their representative. I dabbled in hedonism but was quick to see that the pursuit of pleasure as the chief goal would always leave you hungry, was only an easy way to illusion. Then came Jean-Paul Sartre. Existentialism had become a fashionable philosophy in the postwar years. Be brave, surrender to facts; everything is purposeless, uncertain. Should we not just give up? The playwright Wolfgang Borchert's cry echoed in the emptiness of the prison globe: "Is there no answer?"

Also it was a time of insecurity, a time of disillusion. On the surface an "ism" would appear to be the answer but on closer examination it always crumbled in my hand like a piece of sedimentary rock. There seemed to be no answer to the meaning of life and death, nothing that could give one inner peace and joy.

Then I met H. Deeply affected by the questions and chaos of the war years, he was studying Lutheran theology. He was able to help me to eventually find my own vocation. He awakened me to what love really meant. His tenderness, due to painful disappointments, was unexpectedly cautious. It was he who showed me that one's own self could only be found by turning toward another. For me that has remained the central truth in my life, the center of my Christian experience. No "ism" can give an answer to the problems of life. Only the *you* can. I have never been able to forget this experience, this truth. H. taught it to me.

I came across a small group of colleagues who were Christians and I attended their meetings. I found much of it rather ordinary, most of it strange. But I continued to search. Finally, it happened. There was an old lady from Holland. She used to speak such dreadful German, and I could not help laughing at her quaint phraseology. Then I came to know that she had been an inmate of a German concentration camp and was in Germany to spread the message of love and reconciliation. That made her credible in my eyes. To my question on how one could actually *be* a Christian she simply replied, "One must pray." It happened without my praying—she must have done it for me in my stead. As I walked down the stairs I had to laugh. It was so easy. So convincing. So elating. So very different. So much like falling in love.

> When I came across a passage from John of Damascus—"The divine is incomprehensible and infinite; and this only is comprehensible about it: the infinity and the incomprehensibility"—I felt that the long search for inner peace was beginning to come to an end. I had found my way.

In 1951 I was baptized in the Lutheran Student Congregation. However, my membership in the group was only for a short duration. I was looking for more objectivity, more solid theology, and at the same time something less drab. So I continued my search.

In the midst of all this confusion I made friends with some Roman Catholics. I was impressed by their sympathy toward their neighbor and their sense of humor. Catholicism was certainly not drab, and I began to find it fascinating. I became more familiar with it only after much intensive questioning and study. One of the things that first helped convince me was its emphasis on mysticism, amply expressed by a saying by Thomas Aquinas: "Man will never be able to grasp even the essence of a single mosquito." I immersed myself in theological writings. When I came across a passage from John of Damascus—"The divine is incomprehensible and infinite; and this only is comprehensible about it: the infinity and the incomprehensibility"—I felt that the long search for inner peace was beginning to come to an end. I had found my way.

The all-or-nothing outlook had always been deeply ingrained in my character. So the decision to enter an order was probably a logical conclusion to conversion to Roman Catholicism. I once asked the Jesuit who had received me into the church whether he thought that I had a vocation to the religious life. He replied that although he would not like to rule it out, he thought I should give the question of marriage serious thought and review the situation after a year. "One whole year," I said, "and if the man of my dreams hasn't crossed my path, and I still think of entering an order, can I take it to mean that I have a vocation?" Father K. thought that although it may not have been the most elegant pact, I should certainly not shelve the idea either. So I decided to wait and see. As we were both standing in the doorway I said to him, "My heart has never been able to find satisfaction. Perhaps it shall find it within the church."

The idea that after a year's waiting I would be certain about my life's commitment gave me a certain elation. Quietly I added a secret clause to the pact: If I did meet the man of my dreams and I still wanted to enter an order, would that not be even better?

It was the year in which I met G. I remember the exact time and the glorious feeling. I was doing my practical year in a hospital in Winterberg, he was studying in Marburg, two hundred kilometers (about 124 miles) away. He came every weekend.

G. and I had much in common. With someone else I would not have been able to see it through. In the beginning I was a little uncertain about how I should shape the relationship so that both of us could be free. I said to myself, "It is not a question of my loving him too much or even too little; the question is more as to whether I am capable of loving everyone else with the same intensity." I tried to show a similar concern to my co-workers and to the patients. Often, when somebody dragged me out of bed at night for an emergency, I would ask myself, "How would you react if you were called out to attend to G.?" I loved him because he never treated me as an object, as something to be owned. He was prepared to keep his love in check in order to leave me free to be myself, to find my own way, my unique calling. It was not the case of me being completely rectilinear or living without doubts. For one complete year I lived with one foot here and another there. Once, when saying goodbye, G. said, "Your smile makes me so insecure. I think its roots must be imbedded in something quite beyond our mutual affection."

Then the evening came when G. finally asked me. I listened, aloof, strange, and with unexpected certainty: "Yes, I'd love to … I'd really love to say yes to the marriage, but I can't. I have a vocation, a calling to religious life, and there is no way out but to follow it." And he? Somehow or other he already knew about this glass wall that separated us.

We walked all night through the forest. By morning the certainty had become irrevocable. The secret clause added to the pact had come true. And I have never, never doubted that my decision was right. As he took me to the station at 5 a.m. I told him the story of the secret clause.

When I had decided on principle to enter a religious order my spiritual director said something that I did not forget. He told me it was important to enter the *right* order. He said it was just as important as choosing which man to marry.

There are numerous orders for women, some are contemplative and enclosed. All of them follow a rule and a community life, an abridgement of the rule laid down by St. Anthony the Great of Egypt, who founded the Christian monastic life in 285 CE. Together with the rule are the obligatory vows of poverty, chastity, and obedience.

I decided to join the Daughters of the Heart of Mary, a community following the Jesuit rule of St. Ignatius Loyola. This order emerged during the French Revolution in the 1790s as a kind of religious underground movement. The idea of women who did not live in seclusion, did not wear a nun's habit, but lived with sacred vows in a secular world was new to the church of those days. The idea appealed to me and seemed full of exciting possibilities. I was a doctor. This order was committed to working against misery, wherever it was in the world and with the support and background of a community.

My spiritual director gave me some valuable advice: "When you make your novitiate, take your vow as final. And say to the Lord, 'If you want me out you will have to shoot me out with a cannon.'" This was important. When one is actually "in," it goes without saying that one must accept all that is dreary and commonplace, all that is not part of one's grandiose visions. Membership of a religious order is a union, and like marriage, it is for life.

4

Vocation-Calling

My Vocation

Often when a Muslim and a Westerner talk, the Muslim feels that the Westerner treats him somewhat condescendingly. The Westerner just talks politics or business and rarely touches on the real issues of life—on metaphysical and philosophical matters. The average Muslim finds this rather bewildering. Pakistan is a deeply religious country and any real communication here must be based on this deeper level of metaphysics. However, this depth of faith is seldom found nowadays in any Western society. Even if it is there, it is not expressed

I feel that my acceptance here is due to my being on a similar wavelength as my Muslim friends. A Muslim can understand that my vocation is a symbol of the reality and importance of this transcendental, spiritual aspect in my life, in the life of us all. A Muslim can understand that, for me, forsaking the greatest happiness in this life—to marry and bear children—is indisputable proof that the glory of God and his kingdom are the most concrete, most overpowering realities in my life. In Islamic society a woman can best fulfill herself through marriage and raising her family. I have opted to not have my own children in order to adopt as my own those people who are rejected and outcast, such as leprosy patients. Thus a vocation is a kind of spiritual motherhood. This explains one of the vows I have taken: the vow of chastity.

Now to explain the remaining vows, obedience and poverty. Obedience is a discipline and is symbolic of one's obedience to God, and obedience comes from love. My vow of poverty gives me the possibility to live in solidarity with the poor. It also has its economic advantages as no one has to pay me for the work I do. Thus everyone is able to consult me in my capacity as a foreign expert.

Islam is a grassroots religion. It is a religious and political system, which has taken root in a basically tribal society. In Sharia law, a Muslim has guidelines from God by which to live his life. I often think it may be easier to live my religious vocation in a Muslim society where people believe in God quite naturally, where metaphysical facts are facts, rather than in a secularized, problem-ridden Western country.

The monotheistic religions of Islam and Christianity have much in common. The dividing line is not so much Christianity and Islam but a materialism that makes life so hollow and superficial. To lead a humane existence human beings must have a transcendental dimension, which gives us something more than a mere existence as glorified animals. We must worship something other than ourselves. With this background I am happy to find friends in Pakistan who believe in God, who are able to pray openly without feeling self-conscious and embarrassed.

> To lead a humane existence human beings must have a transcendental dimension, which gives us something more than a mere existence as glorified animals. We must worship something other than ourselves.

I spent one year of my novitiate in an enclosed convent in Paris (I was still a novice when I left for Karachi). The novitiate is a three-year period for spiritual training. As a rule we are designated for civil work or a profession. I had completed my medical studies and my internship before I went to the general novitiate for a year. It was a wonderful time during which I was able to catch up on a lot of reading.

Was my decision correct? Judging by the consequences I can say yes. I had tried to decide according to my best knowledge and conscience. I had tried to see all sides seriously and equally. At the end of this period I took the three vows of chastity, obedience, and poverty. But what does my vow of obedience actually mean to me? Certainly it has made me more tolerant. It has taught me not to bicker over things that are relatively unimportant. Giving in to nonessential issues is undoubtedly easier on the nerves and a habit that can be acquired. It has certainly taught me that one can live with conflicts and still be able to see things from two sides; that peace within tension can still be experienced as peace, that every renunciation, each victory over egoism, leads to an increase in freedom and peace, that inner peace we long for.

Inner freedom, this has always fascinated me in others. Let's look at Helen, for example.

A Sufi in the Desert

Helen came as a volunteer to Pakistan at the age of fifty, during the time of the literacy campaign. She was a remarkable looking woman. Helen was a secretary in the United States and offered her services to Pakistan as a primary school teacher. Later on she entered our order. She too is a convert and we quickly became friends. She too had a rather colorful past before becoming a Catholic. For seven years we lived in the same room in the hospital. We hit it off beautifully during the pioneer period. But as conditions improved she thought that ideals were being betrayed. One day she came to me and said that she wanted to leave Karachi. She was not specialized in anything and I did not know where I could place her. Then, by chance, there was a possibility for her to move to a rather remote station on the Makran coast, inhabited by fishermen. She did not understand a word of Balochi at the time but I thought it was important to have a woman in this far-flung place.

After a year I visited her. No foreigner was allowed to live in this area, with the exception of Helen. Almost as soon as I arrived I was greeted by a delegation of fishermen. They were terribly sorry, they said, but someone had burgled Helen's house. Not that they had anything against burglars, they said, but to rob such a saintly person as Helen, well, that was going positively too far!

When she is asked her age she replies, "Between seventy and one hundred." The older she is, the more respect she receives. Her special charisma is social work among the village women. If a husband beat any of one of them, Helen lets the poor man have it.

She gets a tiny pension, but converted into rupees it is a sizable amount. With this money she is able to help local people, especially women, with their difficulties. She gives the children English lessons. Those children who are unable to go to primary school are taught how to read and write. She also feeds any stray cats.

She paid for a water connection to her house, and whenever the water comes through the pipes—twice a day—she sees that the women of the neighborhood with their pitchers form a neat queue and take their ration one by one so that water is not spilled in an otherwise unavoidable battle to be first. Invariably, when the queue is finished, the water is finished, and it is always Helen who is left without her share.

I still remember that water in Helen's house had been chronically in short supply, which did not induce her in any way to change the mode of distribution! When you lived with Helen, you had to learn to do with less.

A wonderful happy woman, she helps the local leprosy technician by examining the female patients. When he is on tour she keeps his wife company. She leads a varied, rewarding life. When she comes to Karachi, we get ice cream every day—morning, noon, and night. Helen loves ice cream and in Balochistan, where she is, there is none available. Some admirers actually attempted to make some for her. I was there when someone produced a poisonous-looking concoction, which they called ice cream. They thought she would be delighted, and Helen was! But she did not eat it. Daud, the leprosy technician accompanying me, and I had to eat it all, with deadly dismay. Then we took back the empty plate to the suppliers of the noxious fare and said that Helen found it absolutely delicious.

> One can live with conflicts and still be able to see things from two sides; that peace within tension can still be experienced as peace, that every renunciation, each victory over egoism, leads to an increase in freedom and peace, that inner peace we long for.

How often have we pleaded with Helen to return to Karachi! But she too is in the place that the Almighty wants her to be. And I believe that she, more than any of us, has finally found something and, unfettered by the chains that bind us to worldly commitments, has caught a glimpse of eternity in those star-filled Makran nights. With Helen there is no hypocritical depreciation of self, but a vision of God and a humbling experience in loving the poor, the suffering, and the leprosy patients for whom she has sacrificed her life. An ascetic endeavor? Perhaps, yes. But an ascetic endeavors to respond to love for love, for there is no other way to respond.

Jeannine's Love

There are people like Helen, people like Jeannine, who seem to have the ability to attract others because they radiate something, a message our materialistic world is longing for.

Jeannine has already discovered *her* big love: women's rights, education for the underprivileged. Somehow in the midst of a multitude of activities, assisting in the training of leprosy technicians, fieldwork, and being matron of the hospital, Jeannine began to gather a group of girls together and started a prematriculation education program. She concentrated on girls from poor backgrounds and with no prospect in life other than an early marriage and childbearing interspersed with working in the fields. Over the years Jeannine was able to guide many of these girls and help in providing suitable employment upon completion of their studies. Many of them are now nurses in the leading hospitals of Karachi or schoolteachers in their native villages.

Jeannine then carried the dream further. By getting involved in an education program for poorer members of the staff and their children,

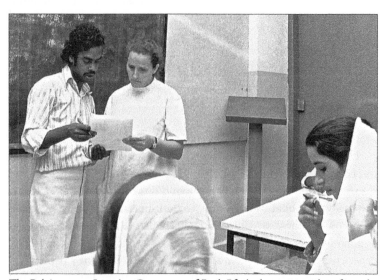

The Belgian nurse Jeannine Geuns, one of Ruth Pfau's closest co-workers from the earliest days of the McLeod Road Dispensary, here teaching trainees, future compounders, in the MALC training room. Photo: DAHW, Hans Kutnewsky

as well as for young discharged leprosy patients, Jeannine made education for the underprivileged a reality with the establishment of an education program for girls and boys. Students are given training within the hospital and on passing the necessary matriculation examination. They are then able to complete further studies such as the leprosy technician course or to find suitable, salaried employment in any of the hospitals or health centers in the country.

It was not long before Jeannine's program had outgrown the boundaries of the leprosy control program, with its necessary rules, ensuring that the team concentrated on the essentials and got the job done.

I, too, often felt that there was so much need around and so many restrictions. Was there really no possibility just to help unconventionally in the most urgent cases, especially when it involved women?

It was a tremendous enrichment for the entire program when Jeannine decided to create her own infrastructure: move out of the hospital, take the risk, and gain the freedom.

Actually, I do not think that Jeannine *decided*. Jeannine does not plan, does not decide, and does not count. She follows the dictates of her heart, and her heart shows the way. Then she goes "to the end." I often remember her thoughtful phrase: "Ruth, don't take anyone on if you do not first make up your mind to *go to the end*."

Jeannine, in the short span of fourteen years, established an incredible number of education and social services. This includes a school for the underprivileged where today more than six hundred and sixty children study: 36 percent from leprosy families or leprosy patients themselves; children of Afghan refugees, picked out of the hopeless misery of the illegal settlements—more garbage heaps than human inhabitation; children of Christian street cleaners; and finally children from normal middle-class or lower-middle-class families who are glad to have found a possibility of having their children educated in one of the good schools of downtown Manghopir. Boys and girls, Shia and Sunni, Christians and Hindus, sick and healthy, Balochis, Pathans, Afghans, Sindhi, Muhajir (Indian immigrants)—children have no problems making friends over the boundaries their adult role models develop!

Next came the resettlement of a group of Hindu families living under inhuman conditions on the garbage heaps of the Lyari riverbank. Here, a housing program, school, primary health post, community development program, microcredit program for the women—an entire community development program started to give back the dignity to these runaway Hindu families.

An embroidery center (which, to our surprise, turned out to be financially viable in no time!), a leather workshop, an interest-free loan program for housing and family emergencies, and an open door for human rights cases when they involved women—all these services were based at the school in Manghopir.

When the illegal Afghan refugees flooded Karachi after the attack of the Americans with their indiscriminate bombing, it was Jeannine who offered her infrastructure for the semilegal emergency help we started, until we convinced the United Nations High Commissioner for Refugees (UNHCR), an international refugee organization, to recognize these Afghans, too.

And when a number of social cases, mostly families with seriously ill members, fell through the UNHCR net, it was Jeannine who somehow scratched together the money to build an Afghan ward at the top of her kindergarten building, where we are still working today for these forgotten victims of an inhuman war.

It is only recently that we put our minds and our ingenuity to tackle the question of sustainability. Since then, Jeannine, too, embarked on the adventure of "handing over."

Jeannine's enthusiasm and energy in organizing was inspiring for us all, especially for the group struggling to secure a future for the program.

5

More Than a Sickness

Caring for People

"Leprosy," wrote Dr. Ashfaq on the blackboard in his beautiful copper-plate handwriting. Then I saw him dramatically crossing out the word.

"I have never seen any leprosy before," he announced to his surprised students. Perplexed silence. Then movement in the second row. Up stood Jamal Khan. "True," he said with a sly smile, "neither have I. I've only seen leprosy bacilli and leprosy patients." Laughter. Then Yaseen said, seriously, "Therefore we should always remember that we are not treating a sickness, we are caring for people."

> We should always remember that we are not treating a sickness, we are caring for people.

When one is speaking medically about the disease, these wise words should be kept in mind. Leprosy is an infectious disease caused by a bacterium related to mycobacterium tuberculosis. Leprosy is not hereditary. It is considerably less infectious than tuberculosis. The earlier the disease is diagnosed, the better the chance of a complete cure. Today leprosy can be, in all stages, brought under control. Of the 15 to 20 million leprosy patients we had in the world since 1985, barely five million are still in need of treatment today. In Pakistan, the figures are even more favorable: of the 50,970 registered patients, not more than 1,100 are still (as of 2003) suffering from an active disease.

We owe this success to the powerful combination treatment, which became available in 1983.

But with this, the menace of leprosy is not yet at the end. About seven hundred thousand new leprosy patients are detected annually worldwide, and about eight hundred of these are in Pakistan. And millions of "cured" leprosy patients are awaiting rehabilitation.

The symptoms of leprosy are: loss of feeling, pale or reddish patches on the skin, and swollen, tender nerves. The incubation period is three to five to even forty years. This means that even when the last infectious leprosy case has been diagnosed, leprosy control measures must still be continued for another two generations. With the multidrug regimen introduced 1984, the treatment period has been dramatically reduced from ten years to six months for noninfectious cases and from lifelong to two years for infectious cases. However, even cured cases must be periodically reexamined for a considerable length of time.

If left untreated, leprosy is an ugly, frightening disease. It destroys the body gradually, ever so gradually, when nothing is done about it. Initially it begins with an innocent-looking light-colored patch on the skin. When pricked with a pin there is no sensation of pain. The first stage is a lack of feeling.

I still remember the seemingly hopeless struggle in the early days of the McLeod Road Dispensary. In the night the rats used to crawl through the holes in the huts and gnaw away at any exposed anaesthetic hands or feet. No cut is felt, no pain, because the nerves are numb.

Even more monstrous than the danger of increasing disfigurement is society's attitude toward the leprosy patient. The panicking fear of infection. The groundless stigmatizing of patients as sinners, struck by a scourge of God. At first it is possible to cover up the disease. A salwar kameez can hide a lot. But slowly, the small, pale patches grow larger. As the nerves get affected a leg wastes away, an arm rots. With leprosy, death comes slowly. Leprosy does not kill directly; it destroys

In the slum of Karachi, a leprosy patient, who in the early days of the McLeod Road Dispensary could only be treated with painkillers.

our warning sense of pain, leading to painless injuries and pus infections that may poison the blood.

For centuries the leprosy patient was isolated from society. Today it is no longer necessary because leprosy is curable. But there is still prejudice, even among those who should know better. There was an example many years back in the colony. A young Pakistani doctor wanted to help but only under the condition that nobody was told about it. He would have lost his job if he were discovered to be working among leprosy patients. Once in the early 1960s, a patient came to me with such terrible blood poisoning that an operation was required immediately. I ran all over the place looking for a surgeon. Eventually, through the telephone directory, I found an orthopedic specialist who was also a surgeon. On meeting him I shook his hand in the German style. He immediately rushed to the washbasin and washed his hands thoroughly. I had told him that I worked with leprosy patients. Surely just a reflex. He did not want to offend me personally. I also remember a Pakistani woman doctor who was suffering from leprosy. On discovering the nature of her illness she had a nervous breakdown, even though she was in an early stage, which was easily curable. I was actually afraid that she would commit suicide. We invited her to dinner. I "accidentally" took her drinking glass and drank from it so that she would notice, to show her that we were not afraid of leprosy. During the next visit she said, "I have read everything about leprosy but it is just not enough to sweep away all the horrors of my childhood. I was the youngest in the family and was always allowed to give the alms to the beggars who used to come to the garden gate. Once, when I was giving some coins to one, my mother came rushing up, screaming in panicky fear: 'Don't you know that you mustn't go near him!' He had leprosy. This has stuck so deeply in my mind that all the textbooks on leprosy in the world can't rid me of it."

Walled In

A truly shocking fate befell Adina, a fourteen-year-old girl from the far north of Pakistan. Adina was kept prisoner in a cave for two years by the people of her village, just because she had leprosy. The cave was only two paces wide. In front they had constructed a high stonewall. Her father had thrown her, his own daughter, out of the house. The family and villagers had walled her up in this cave in a village at a short distance from the Chitral border. We found her there in 1980.

I climbed onto a stone to look down into the cave. The wall was much too high. It was a total loss. I did not know what to do.

"Climb over it," Abdullah, the leprosy technician who was with me, said coolly. He never thought that a problem was insurmountable. But over that wall? How?

How I ever managed, I do not know. I reached the top and looked down into the cave. I caught sight of a head bobbing back and forth, and then it was gone. I leaned over as far as I could and stretched my hand over the wall. It was tightly clasped by a cold little hand from the other side. Good, I thought, nonverbal communication seems to work. I jumped, and then Adina was in my arms. She was a young girl, hardly fourteen, half naked and shivering in the cold. I took off my pullover, she pulled it on with obvious delight; it reached down to her knees.

I found a sweet in my pocket. "*Dawai* (medicine)," she said seriously, and began obediently to swallow it, complete with paper wrapping. I laughed and unwrapped it for her. I managed to find three more and she wolfed them down with the same greed. "*Mithai* (sweet)," she corrected herself happily. And that was our first conversation. Then I began her medical checkup.

The meeting with the villagers was rather stormy. About twelve men sat in a circle, the *numberdar* (policing authority) with the village elders and the father. We explained the facts about leprosy and demanded that the girl be taken back into the family. There was an atmosphere of hostility and irrational fear. We talked and talked—in Urdu, in Sheena, in Koar—until Abdullah lost his temper: "If you don't want her," he shouted, "then give her to me!" Silence. Then unanimous consent.

Abdullah was unusually businesslike, cool and efficient. He got the father to sign that he gave permission for the girl to be taken away, and the village *numberdar* to countersign as witness. "What will you do with her?" I asked. He looked up for a moment, bewildered. Then he smiled. "My mother will take her," he said. "There are already seven of us at home, so what difference will one more make?"

It took us four days to reach Gilgit. Adina was only able to take four steps at a time before wanting to sit down and rest. Once Abdullah burst out, "You were born here in the mountains and you can't even walk for half a mile without taking a rest!" And she, quick as a flash, replied, "You just sit for two years in a cave!" We all laughed. Finally, we made it to the jeep. I sat in the front seat, Adina in my arms, warm, contented, excited, and enjoying herself at every turn and jolt the jeep made on the dangerous, narrow, stony road down the valley.

Such a precious booty. "And if we would not have found her," said Abdullah in a pensive moment, "before the valley was snowbound, what would have happened?" "But we did find her," I said. "God is good!"

Death Sentence in the Valley

It was 1982. We were on tour in Ranikot with a German television team. Our equipment was transported by camel. The cameleer told us the history of leprosy in the area.

He still could remember, fifteen to twenty years ago, as the news swept through the valley like a bushfire. A tribesman was suffering from leprosy. When the fact became known, access to the village wells was forbidden to him, which was a death sentence for the man and his flocks on this arid, stony plateau. He and his family were banished to the far-thest corner of the valley, from which there was no way out. There, the poor fellow and his family managed to exist by the side of a small, almost dried-up well. One must first see the wells in Ranikot in order to comprehend the fear and exhaustion that the family must have had to endure. Finally, the sheer will to survive drove them to the near impos-sible: to bore the well shaft deep enough to strike ground water.

At that time, we knew nothing about Ranikot, the Gabol Baloch, and their problems. The banished tribesman had already died before our team reached the valley. In the meantime, the son had become infected and it had developed into an infectious form of leprosy. We arrived just in time. His nine-year-old son was diagnosed as an early case, and in the following year was discharged as completely cured. Finally, the widow of the first leprosy patient showed early symptoms of the disease. In the near future she will be discharged from treatment too.

Since Fateh Mohammad summoned his final strength in digging the well, the situation in the valley had fundamentally changed. In the past three years only early cases have been discovered. During the last tour we thoroughly combed the area and found only two cases, both in the very early stages. Today it is possible to talk about the disease openly and to come openly for treatment. Everyone in Ranikot knows from personal experience that leprosy is curable. The ban on marriage with leprosy patients, which was imposed by the tribe, has been lifted. Nevertheless, this happy development applies only to the valley of Ranikot. As we were combing the neighboring valleys during this tour (and they are still much less accessible), during one day alone we found six new cases of untreated leprosy.

Hashim

Hashim grew up in a fishing village by the Arabian Sea. It is a village locked in between the endlessness of the ocean and the ever-stretching desert of sand and rocks. In the flank of a rock reef there is a freshwater well and there the life of the village revolves, as it also does around the fleet of fishing boats.

Sublime, hostile, and remote, these are the features common to sea and desert. Whoever has the misfortune to be ostracized from the village community must face the menaces of sea and desert.

Hashim fell ill when he was only six. By the time he had reached eight, the disease could not be hidden anymore. His bloated face, his shapeless ears, the ulcers on his hands and feet—for everybody, easily recognizable; for everybody, a living advertisement.

His mother tried her best to hide the lad in the house. But who can keep such a secret in a village of only twenty or thirty huts, where everyone knows the other? "I still remember when we were youngsters and used to drive poor Hashim away with stones." This was told to me twelve years later by one of the villagers who was of the same age group as Hashim and grew up with him.

The fact could no longer be concealed, pressure came from all sides, and in the end the villagers resorted to the only sentence known to them: ostracism. The fisher-folk with whom Hashim lived took him far into the desert, to an area so inhospitable and forbidding that any chance of return could never have been imagined. There was only the ceaseless howl of the wind and the fury of the biting sand. And the sun, like a fiery sentinel above. In this desolation the eldest brother erected a tiny mud hut for the child and promised to bring him water and food. That was only possible, however, when there was no sandstorm. As Hashim watched his brother disappear over the sand-swept horizon, he remembered the monotonous frequency of the sandstorms.

One day the boy was spotted in the village, in the area where the catch was auctioned from the returning fishing boats. After that, there was no sign of him again. His brother rushed to the place where Hashim had been abandoned. The hut was empty and lay in ruins. The village folk who used to sit around the fire on the beach, spinning yarns long into the night, told any returning fishermen the story of how Hashim had met the same fate as other leprosy patients before him; that the wild animals had done what the community felt unable to do. And the fishermen listened spellbound as the grisly story unfolded. In the brief silences, as they contemplated the awful reality, they heard only the pounding of the waves on the shore and the crackle of the fire.

Hashim never told me how, as a mere child, he must have suffered during those long, lonely nights in the desert. Whenever I used to try to bring the subject up he would always signal me to stop. "God has been good to me," he used to say. "He has brought me to Karachi and here I have found another mother." Actually, a camel caravan had found the half-unconscious youngster somewhere in the desert and somehow he turned up in Karachi—just how he still cannot remember. I also cannot remember how we found him.

> I still recall how I could no longer bring myself to
> simply stand by and see how the pain brought
> the youngster to the borders of despair

When he was admitted, he was so ravaged by the disease that I thought at the time that he must have been an old man. He did not know any Urdu nor I any Balochi; at the same time any form of conversation between us would have been impossible. He was too ill, and I was too tense. The lad had developed a serious kidney complication and there seemed little hope of his recovery.

I cannot understand how he managed to survive when so many of my patients suffering from the last stages of the disease died. Hashim himself had the answer: "God's will." Even we doctors could not come up with a counterargument.

I still recall how I could no longer bring myself to simply stand by and see how the pain brought the youngster to the borders of despair, and how I, in a last desperate attempt, decided to put him on cortisone. To calm my conscience I tried to believe that there would not be enough time left for any side effects to occur.

And now? Hashim has gone off on his honeymoon. "I never dared to hope," he said, as he bade me farewell, "that fortune could also be on my side, and now look." The day that he was declared cured he celebrated with a party—garlands for the doctors and tea for the staff. Six weeks later he announced his engagement. He used to receive a modest but regular wage as a hospital ward boy. Then came the greatest moment of his life. At that time we set out on our first survey expedition to Makran, where he came from. We took Hashim along as interpreter. After twelve long years, he was homeward bound.

In the second week we reached Sur, that forsaken fishing village in which Hashim's story began. Dust-laden, thirsty, and exhausted, we stumbled into a house that belonged to a village elder. We were received

Departing the MALC outpost in Balochistan to survey the desert region of Makran, with Daud, a leprosy field officer (the radiator of Land Rover), and considerable quantities of medical supplies. Photo: DAHW, Hans Kutnewsky

with true Islamic hospitality. He provided us with a room for our medical supplies, our mobile outpatient department. Any leprosy cases in the district? No, nothing at all. He recalled that ten or fifteen years ago there was the youngest son of Ruzi ... what was his name? "Hashim," piped up Hashim, who was standing with us. Did he know him? (Surely, that face was familiar, he thought.) "Yes," he replied. "It is me."

The news spread throughout the village like wildfire. Hashim, son of Ruzi, had come back—*cured*. Impossible! But yes, here he was, a foreign doctor's assistant and in Muhammad Ali's house for all to see.

There was a right royal banquet that evening and the whole village turned up. Hashim was given the place of honor and drank from the same jug that was handed around the circle of seated fisher-folk. And Hashim had to tell the story of his cure over and over again. Then, in the same evening, three patients who had previously concealed their disease came forward for treatment. In the morning we found two more. From then on the ice had been broken. Whenever we arrived in a village along the coastal strip, the news that our medicine could cure leprosy always preceded us. We had living proof with us. Everyone could recognize the face that had been believed dead. We opened two centers in the area, a district in which one hundred and forty patients are under treatment.

To Change a Life, a Country

Mahatma Gandhi, who was a great friend of leprosy patients, once said:

> Leprosy work is not merely medical relief; it is transforming the frustration of life into the joy of dedication, personal ambition into selfless service. If you can transform the life of a patient or change his values of life, you can change the village and the country.

I can subscribe to that.

Originally I had no particular specialist interests in leprosy; it just developed. Leprosy is a very interesting field of medicine but that alone was not enough to motivate me. For me, the fascinating thing about leprosy is that one has a lifelong association with one's patients. When someone has malaria, he comes, he is healed, and one does not usually see him again. The patients, whose children we delivered into the world some twenty-five to thirty years ago, are grandparents today, who will still come and proudly present their grandchildren to us and tell us all of the family history, which finally took a happy turn once this baby had arrived and all the ill feelings vanished!

The difficulty in achieving *leprosy elimination*, after leprosy control had been achieved in 1986, lies in organizational problems. As mentioned earlier, leprosy has an incubation period of three to five to even forty years. Annually, we are still finding about eight hundred new patients in Pakistan, and seven hundred thousand worldwide. On average, we have access to about 50 percent of the funds formerly available to us, before the World Health Organization (WHO) declared leprosy *controlled* and struck Pakistan from the list of endemic countries. For a moment we were proud, but then even more upset. What is *leprosy*? Bacilli in the body and the adequate or inadequate answer of the immune system to this invading germ. Or is leprosy the reaction of a human person, a family, a community to a disease that is so misunderstood? "Cure": Is this not rather a process that gives the patient back his lost dignity so that he can earn, marry, send his children to school, live with equal rights in society—whatever these "rights" are in a society like Pakistan? We discharge a patient only when he has access to those seven human rights we consider his birthright: the right to food and clothing, shelter, education for himself and his children, access to basic health services, social acceptance, and equal rights in the labor market.

Although a clinical cure for leprosy is possible today in six months to two years, a long-term surveillance of the patient is necessary to prevent relapse. This is bound to result in a generation-long relationship with the patient and his whole family

How did we tackle the leprosy endemic in Pakistan? When I arrived in Pakistan in 1960, I had no proper specialist training in leprosy. I only acquired this later in India. Analyzing the problems and possibilities, we then put the program together, step by step, ensuring it was equally concerned with combating the disease and in helping patients.

When we moved into our hospital in 1963 we began compiling statistics. They showed us that most of the patients consistently came from the same areas. That meant it would be worthwhile to find every region where leprosy was endemic. These were Balochistan, the North-West

Frontier Province, Azad Kashmir, and Northern Areas. A considerable number of men from these provinces used to migrate to industrialized Karachi at the onset of winter. These seminomads made up a large number of our patients in the sixties. In 1971 and 1972, refugees from the former Eastern Wing were added.

Then, from 1982 to 1985, came refugees from Afghanistan, including a wave of highly advanced patients with stages of leprosy we had not seen for decades in Pakistan.

The second wave of refugees came after the American forces attacked Afghanistan and fought their war ruthlessly with carpet bombing. The misery of these families, who had to flee their homes during the winter, was beyond anything we could imagine.

In Pakistan? I really have to remember how it all began.

We simply started where we found need and where we saw a possibility—and trusted that the government would be impressed with our results. And so it happened: in 1965, we started in the North-West Frontier Province; in 1968 in Azad Kashmir and Northern Areas; in 1971 in Balochistan; in 1978 in Sindh. Additionally, in 1984 we decided to go, illegally, into Soviet-occupied Afghanistan. Now we want to do the same for tuberculosis patients, to control a disease that still claims so many lives.

I went for the first time to the northern provinces in 1965 with the superior of our Karachi convent. The outcome of the visit was the discovery that many of the patients who came to us from the provinces had family members who also suffered from leprosy. The women and children who stayed behind had no treatment facilities and were unable to make a journey to the city, not only because of poverty but also because of *purdah*, which means in Islamic cultures the restriction of women to the house. *We* had to go to the *people*; we had to train paramedical workers. In 1965 we started to train future leprosy technicians, the first batch to be trained in Pakistan. A core group did not exist. We created the first posts of leprosy technicians in North-West Frontier Province in 1968. The six-month course included leprosy diagnosis, therapy, complications and their management, record keeping, statistics, and English. Now the course is for two years and includes physics, chemistry, anatomy, public health practice, communication skills, as well as a detailed study of leprosy and related subjects, including the treatment and prevention of common diseases in Pakistan, with an emphasis on tuberculosis. Physiotherapy for leprosy patients, compounding, nursing, and social work are taught as well. On completion of the course the leprosy technicians return to their districts and take over the management of the leprosy centers established by the provincial governments. They have consulting hours for outpatients, and are touring the district by motorcycle, jeep, bus, camel, and frequently by foot. Under the most exhausting conditions, they search out new cases and look after registered patients, delivering medicines and contacting family and community. In 1968, the Marie Adelaide Leprosy Center team gave the central government in Islamabad a detailed plan for a National Leprosy Control Program, which would include all provinces as well as Greater Karachi. Of course, all this planning and negotiating with the government has taken much time. Report writing has never been my preferred occupation, though I spend a lot of time doing it by necessity. But sometimes we do it even voluntarily. Sometimes we have to reassure ourselves that it has been worthwhile, that much has happened. And for this we have a comparison chart that we update annually:

	1960	2004
Provincial Programs	0	5
NGOs	3	5
Leprosy Technicians	0	351

The step-by-step tasks of the General Health Service were also included in the program. By 1985 we already had nearly 200 employees in Karachi. In addition, 115 government employees rendered various services in the most far-flung corners of the land. There were 30,000 registered leprosy patients located over 347,000 square kilometers—30,000 men, women, and children who had only one hope: these small white tablets brought by the leprosy technician. In 1975 we have started to treat tuberculosis in Azad Kashmir and we established a program for blindness prevention in Balochistan. The blindness program was later initiated in the Northern Areas and in the North-West Frontier Province.

6

The Enrichment Flows
from One to Another

Understanding Is Better Than Parroting

One of the most exciting things in life for me is to help someone to self-realization and development. Albertus Magnus, the teacher of the famous philosopher and saint Thomas Aquinas said, "For a teacher there is no greater happiness than being excelled by a pupil." There is a similar aspect in the relationship of parents and children. The same excitement. The enrichment flows from one to another. I am passionately fond of teaching. These lads have already passed the matriculation examination. The school system is often modeled on the Quranic school teaching method, and this means learning by heart. If only they could make a discovery themselves! It mostly takes about six weeks before the first one asks, "Why?" Not long ago I was teaching botany. We had set up a miniature natural science museum. The discovery that one can see in nature, a subject only read about in books, is wonderful.

> One of the most exciting things in life for me is to help someone to self-realization and development.

Although everyone has passed his matriculation, not that it means much these days, they stare in a dumbfounded way when I say "cell." I say "tissue" and they shake their heads. After a number of anatomy lectures I say "nerves" and that seems to strike a light. It is like lighting a candle in the darkness when someone suddenly begins to understand something. I had never realized that teaching could be so creative. But above all, the thing that makes me happiest is to deliberately take someone from the usual routine and encourage him for taking initiatives.

There are lessons like this: They had not yet used their anatomy workbook and, in any case, did not know where to start. They were still sitting obediently at their desks, just like in the good old school days. "The skull consists of two parts: cranium and the facial bones." Book closed. "The skull consists of two parts: the er ... cran ... cranium and the facial bones." Book open.

> To pick someone out, to instill initiative
> and consciousness. To enter into the life
> of another, to lift him out toward broader
> horizons. I had that wonderful feeling then.

We had all colored in three or four pages of different diagrams. "Now look once more, in connection with the text," I said. Blue-blue-blue, red-red-red. Their eyes lit up in comprehension. Ha, the breakthrough! *Naturally*, the temporal bones are over the temporal lobes of the brain— that is why they have the same sort of names. And, naturally, the hearing impressions are stored in the temporal lobes, and then the temporal bone is obviously part of the ear canal! Sudden delight! "And that is why it is so easy for a political chorus with all its slogans to sell you up the riverbed," I remarked dryly.

"The teaching and learning methods," says Qurban Ali with concern, "start in the primary school. The teacher reads"—Qurban takes up a book in imitation—"'The moon is red,' and we all follow in chorus, 'the moon is red.'" "Exactly like that," I say. A concerned silence, then amused grins. Then Saira, the only girl in the class: "Understanding is so *much* better than parroting." Unanimous agreement.

To pick someone out, to instill initiative and consciousness. To enter into the life of another, to lift him out toward broader horizons. I had that wonderful feeling then, that on that day we had learned much more than finding the temporal lobes of the brain under the temporal bone of the skull pan.

Ustad

The fellowship with my boys is worth more than mere training of efficient leprosy technicians. It is an opportunity to raise the level of consciousness, to develop a sense of responsibility. Mostly it comes, inevitably, through the work. Sometimes consciousness can be built in. In Pakistan the teacher-student relationship is similar to the master-pupil relationship. This gives one an enormous influence in the role of *ustad* (teacher).

Our leprosy technicians are the all-important subjects in my life. Perhaps they are so close to my heart because I no longer have quite the same relationship with patients; there are too many of them now. I still can reach them, but only through our technicians. They also carry the torch, guaranteeing that the values that characterize the program are kept alive. We are in constant dialogue, even after work hours. I am able to discuss their relationship with sisters, wives, and daughters, to point out that God has made all people equal, and that this is one of the basic tenets of the Holy Qur'an.

But have we affected any changes yet? Tradition can be unbelievably tenacious. Even when change is inwardly accepted, parental opposition can thwart it.

Dr. Pfau training future leprosy and tuberculosis technicians in the MALC training room. Photo: DAHW, Hans Kutnewsky

Teacher and Pupil—the Bridge Over the Chasm

There is much I have learned from my boys. There is the story of the suspension bridge.

The mountain folk had cut notches in the cliff for foot grips. There was only space for one foot. Far below, the river was hurtling angrily along its turbulent course. Then the other foot had to somehow fit into the aperture above. I was not able to do it alone. I was simply too afraid. This exchange of roles can be a great experience for both sides. This is the role of fieldwork. The driver decides just how far the jeep proceeds and at which point we must all get out and walk. Then the lads from that particular district take over command.

"Don't look down," advised Ibrahim. "Just look at the cliff wall. Now put your foot in here." I felt proud at having completed the climb and was overcome with triumph. As we reached the top of the climb I saw the bridge, a suspension bridge. It is one of the things I am most afraid of. Wooden planks laid over wire ropes. As soon as one sets foot on the thing it begins to sway dizzily over the chasm far below. If one is unfortunate enough to lose balance or move too far to one side, the wooden planks tilt upward. As I stood surveying the sight confronting me I thought it would be crazy to play the hero. I was on the verge of bursting into tears. And this, after having overcome the most difficult part of the ordeal, the long and strenuous cliff climb. "I can't do it. I'll fall off," I said. But, at the same time, we just could not turn back. The patients were all on the other side. Ibrahim dismissed the proposal to call the villagers for help. He found his own solution: "I will carry you over," he said. "Just shut your eyes!" And he picked me up and carried me over the swaying bridge. Of course, I had my eyes firmly shut during the whole operation. As he set me down safely on the other side he laughingly said, "You and your 50 kilos (about 110 pounds). It was quite simple actually." And then, getting serious, "I wouldn't have been able to watch if someone else had done it. If something had gone wrong, then at least both of us would have, er ... become *shaheed!*" We both laughed and began the steep climb down to a patient's house. *Shaheed* means "martyr in holy war."

The Trout Fishers

On the way up to Karakorum we had to cross a glacier that was very much on the move. School children were able to lead us across. On the other side I met a patient who was suffering from acute tuberculosis of the spine. To bring him over the dangerous glacier was out of question. At that time there was an Italian mountaineering expedition in the vicinity. A member of the team had developed hepatitis and was conveyed to the nearest city by helicopter. When I heard this news, I thought, here is that foreigner being evacuated by helicopter and my boys and I must cross all this dangerous ice in our sandals. When we have an emergency we are unable to help, such things can make one furious. One day, after an eighteen-kilometer (about eleven miles) trudge because we had run out of petrol, a helicopter flew low over us. In it was a pair of officials who had flown in for trout fishing. I was almost driven to despair. But what else could one do under such exasperating conditions but just push on. The parable of the Good Samaritan comes to mind in such cases. And the command, "You go then, and do the same!" It means that we should act like a neighbor to those who suffer. It also implies that we should make changes in conditions so that no others fall into danger. Change for the better means, foremost, training more helpers. How many of the nearly thirty thousand patients (in 1985) can be reached by me alone? As none of the roads in those areas is marked on the map, I was at first confused at how to reach the villages on our itinerary. On top of this there are language difficulties. There are many different languages and dialects spoken in Pakistan; we counted forty-six. I may be able to treat our patients but where Urdu is not spoken I can only reach them linguistically through the local leprosy technicians. In reality, these workers are not my *assistants*. It is just the reverse: I assist them.

What Does It Mean—Success?

Leprosy work is the only vehicle that enables me to penetrate Pakistani society. The people for whom I stand, I have no abstract plan for achieving success.

Sometimes what I dream of actually comes true. Once it happened with Hussain, one of the technicians and a former patient who had just been employed by us.

One morning I met Ali on the stairs. "Listen," I said, "is it true that Hussain has applied for that difficult post in Balochistan?"

"Yes, it is true," Ali said. "Rest assured, he's serious about it"

"How?" I asked, "that baby …?"

"He isn't any more," Ali said, and my mind suddenly flashed back to a rather tiring tour in the wilds of Balochistan.

Hussain is a leprosy technician. He had been retrenched by another organization. At the time he applied, I needed a worker for the tour in Balochistan. I told him that he could come along. Hussain began to make excuses. He was still technically a patient, and he would not be able to stand the heat. So much walking would be quite impossible. "But you are thirty years younger than me, and if *I* can do something then you can do even more," I told him. He had never eaten chapatis before, only rice. "And before I came to Pakistan, I had not even seen a chapati," I told him rather impatiently. "Okay, if you want to come, be here by 6:15 tomorrow morning." Hussain came.

By noon we had reached the last district outpost. Then the journey through the desert began. We spent the night in some of the "hotels" on the way—straw huts along the roadside. The team ate chapatis. Hussain had brought along a supply of biscuits. The next day was the same. The team ate chapatis for lunch, Hussain ate biscuits. The evening meal was a repeat performance: chapatis for us, biscuits for him. Then he ran out of biscuits.

It had rained during the day. Crossing a raging torrent of rainwater had cost us more time than we had estimated. There seemed no hope of reaching our goal by evening. A goat shepherd took us into his tent for the night and we shared our woollen blankets. The next morning we discovered that the rain had washed away the road farther along. The jeep bounced over the huge potholes and there was only one padded seat. After every fifty kilometers (about 31 miles) or so we took turns sitting in it.

Hussain had to leave his home when he was a child and his whole life was spent in a leprosarium. He went to school there, he passed his matriculation there, and he found work there. The sisters had done everything for him; he lived a sheltered life, but the life of a *patient*, a life apart. During the Balochistan tour, everything was so different. Everyone shared the blankets at night and his disease was forgotten. On his return, Hussain told me that he could never ever—*never ever*—have dreamed of being treated as a normal person. There was no fuss, no special attention; he was treated just normal, like everyone else. The Balochistan tour had changed his whole life. Hussain gained confidence in himself.

"By all means send him off to Balochistan," Ali said. "He is serious about it."

For the rest of the day I felt rather elated. God is great! We had succeeded in making a patient stand on his own feet, and unintentionally received more in the bargain. Six weeks of unnoticed psychotherapy and the result: a voluntary application for one of the most difficult jobs in Balochistan. I told Hussain that I was happy that he had applied. He told me that he needed a microscope and laboratory equipment and, if possible, a sleeping bag. He wanted the microscope for accurate diagnosis; he did not want to sit around all day in the clinic. He wanted to visit the villages, hence the sleeping bag. I promised to try to obtain both for him. Life had completely unfolded for Hussain and I had hardly noticed the change.

The Archa-Nala Crossing

One of my most rewarding experiences was with Karim, the leprosy technician responsible for the team in Azad Kashmir. One day he insisted on going out on fieldwork even though it was pouring rain. The mountain tracks are of red clay, and in rainy weather they are as slippery as soap. On one side lay the mountain and on the other side an abyss. Every time the jeep slid toward the abyss conversation would automatically stop. When it slid over to the mountainside of the road, Karim would continue it again. After two kilometers (just over a half mile) I inquired, "Karim, is this really necessary?" He replied in the affirmative. Well, he *is* the team leader. I had been racking my brain the whole journey to find out how it was possible that I had trained such an irresponsible team leader. The lives of the whole team were in danger. We could have at least waited one more day. Though it was also possible that if further rain came we would not have been able to get through in any case. We really should have waited, I thought. We were the only vehicle on the road, except for a military patrol, which overtook us to ask why we were traveling in such inclement weather. I replied in a flash, "Karim said we had to go!"

Farther up in the valley there was still a patient to attend to. A stony path led upward to his house. Karim said, "As there are no women in this house you had better stay down here. We have only got to take some medicine up to him and if you come along it will take us a full hour, whereas we can do it in twenty minutes. So why don't you wait?" I waited. On their return, I could see them as they tore down the precipice-like path. It was as if the three of them had taken a bet on who would reach the jeep first. Karim was the winner with the others close behind him. Watching them race down, a suicidal venture, I suddenly had an insight. The determination to set out in such adverse conditions could not be put down to irresponsibility on the part of Karim; it was simply his age. "I am sorry," I said. "I have been griping the whole time. I just couldn't understand you. Just now it clicked." And Karim, with a visible sigh of relief, replied, "I've been wondering all the time why you have been so cross. I was just thinking about when we crossed the Archa-Nala."

The Archa-Nala ... that was many years ago, and during that journey I was team leader. A bridge had been washed away and we had to get to the other side of the river. On that particular day the military had decided not to cross because the water level was too high. We said, "If the army won't take the plunge, the leprosy team will." And so we started to cross the Archa-Nala. Having miraculously escaped a near disaster we reached a rock and I just could not control my tears. I thought that we would never make it. After that I have never done anything like it again.

For Karim, my style was the Archa-Nala crossing. And now, when he is at the age that I was then, and chasing his team over this terrifying stretch, I thought that he was behaving irresponsibly. He had only copied me. He gave me a faint smile. If I ever thought in Muzaffarabad about whether it was safe to move out, you can be sure that I would have not set out at all!

In God's Hands

The saying "in God's hands" must be taken seriously. It was Shamsher who handed me the telegram. I was standing on the fourth floor. It was twenty minutes past eight in the morning. Abdul Salam ... dead.

He was twenty-four years old. Only last year he had completed his leprosy technician's course. He was a lad from the hills, alert, full of enthusiasm, devoted and accustomed to a hard life. He had taken over the most underdeveloped district in Azad Kashmir and had just been made responsible for a leprosy control center because of his good, commendable work.

The accident happened near Noseri. The bus hurled into a ravine. The so-called road from Noseri to Athmuqam and farther on to Sharda and Kehl is nothing more than a suicidal goat path hewn through the mountain. It is only wide enough for a single vehicle. I have often driven along this route, but never without being on the alert. Once I urgently required a signature to an agreement but I did not seem to be making much progress. Then I invited the civil servant concerned with the agreement to Kundal Shahi. To get to Kundal Shahi one has to take the road via Noseri. By chance I steered the conversation onto the agreement, shortly after Noseri. The civil servant only kept absent-mindedly muttering "Yes, yes" to everything I said, his eyes staring fixedly ahead, his hands tightly clenched. In Kundal Shahi I got the long-awaited signature. I finally convinced him that my boys performed a more than ordinary job. But there are hundreds, even thousands of roads in the north that are just as treacherous as the Noseri one. And in spite of all this, the leprosy team has almost always miraculously survived any impending accidents.

We have all lived with the firm conviction that God could not afford to lose us. Everything had always ended up so wonderfully that nobody needed to convince us that we were somewhat special. We knew it.

Once, when we were in a dry riverbed and suddenly surprised by a flash flood, we managed to get through, contrary to all expectations. The villagers said that no one could have survived, but the leprosy team was somewhat special and God could not afford to lose us. Like the Volkswagen bus when it overturned, like the Suzuki jeep as it rolled down a mountain, or the Willy's jeep that nearly bounced over a cliff but came to a halt only inches over the brink—after all this we have all lived with the firm conviction that God could not afford to lose us.

Everything had always ended up so wonderfully that nobody needed to convince us that we were somewhat special. We knew it.

> *And now Abdul Salam*
> *There are so many landslides ...*
> *You knew it ahead.*
> *Why did you not cause an engine breakdown,*
> *which would have kept the bus back?*
> *Why did you let them drive on?*
> *Oh God, you know best. We keep on asking why such*
> *things happen;*
> *but Lord, you know best,*
> *Your will be done.*

In the Name of God, the Beneficent ...

Bashir Mohammad was the first leprosy technician who had not been a leprosy patient. Bashir grew up in a place of pilgrimage famous for its spring water, which, although it did not heal leprosy patients, was thought to stop the progress of the disease. Due to this belief, a group of beggars had settled around the spring. The lad was deeply affected by their plight. He wanted to learn how to cure leprosy, and, with this in mind, bombarded me with letters. At that time there were no treatment facilities in this area. When an itinerant monk moved into the colony and began to do social work among the leprosy patients, Bashir Mohammad made contact with him and, as a result, his determination to learn everything possible about leprosy treatment and to serve the patients grew even stronger. Finally, I let him come down to Karachi. Some of his friends also became interested in this kind of work, and in this way an elite group came into being.

I made up my mind to groom this elitism. At that time leprosy work carried no prestige. Society was apt to pour scorn on anyone who took up work in this field. But in spite of all the odds these technicians dedicated themselves energetically and fought hard to achieve a high social status for this profession. There is a promise to which all leprosy technicians vow to adhere. It is intended to strengthen the moral integrity of the group. They formulated it themselves, basing it on the Hippocratic

Oath. The newly qualified leprosy technicians solemnly promise, in the name of God, the Beneficent, the Merciful, and there follow ten commandments. One of them is to serve the patients with sympathy and understanding, regardless of religious belief, political conviction, race, or social standing. Another is never to harm patients by assuming responsibilities in the field of medicine for which no training has been received. One promises a high professional standard and to be cooperative with colleagues, promoting a team spirit and a sense of brotherhood among those working for the same goal.

All are deeply influenced by religion. It is like the very air that they breathe. Here we are on common ground. At any time I can say without reservation, "You all know that I cannot always watch you, but God is able to see everything."

> All are deeply influenced by religion. It is like
> the very air that they breathe. Here we are
> on common ground…. Purely humanitarian
> motives are not enough to see one through. The
> frustrations, the problems are too numerous.

There is not much money to earn in this field, but this has had little effect on the social prestige enjoyed by the group. It is a dedicated life and their elitist consciousness gives them the confidence to continue against all odds. Whatever holds good for the workers is ultimately good for me, too. Purely humanitarian motives are not enough to see one through. The frustrations, the problems are too numerous. One could almost suffer a breakdown over what one is unable to do.

I admire the way they keep it up. When Abdullah leaves his warm bed on a misty winter morning and ventures out into the snow and biting cold to attend to the patients in their isolated mountain villages, he must be able to draw strength from some spiritual reservoir in order to continue the work so faithfully, so true to the leprosy technician's promise, right up to his tragic and untimely death.

There is an anecdote about Abdullah: The spark plugs in our jeep were burned out and we had no spare ones with us. The only solution was to go ahead on foot and in the meantime send the driver back to try to find some. It was around 4 p.m. when we set out in the mountain districts of Karakorum. I asked Abdullah where we were going to spend the night. "We shall walk until it is dark and then we'll see," he replied. The idea that anything could go wrong never occurred to him, or if did, he did not entertain the thought. We were on a mission and God would see us through. We knew that we were in God's hands. We walked until it became dark. One moment we were worried—and now? Where to go? Then a shepherd took us in.

Service and *Izzat*

Jamal Khan is one of those people who possess great vehemence of feeling "service." He said, "I previously never understood the real meaning of "service," but now!" The following story illustrates this.

A tribe had blocked the road. There had been a dispute with the government and in retaliation they had begun to seize buses, holding the passengers as hostages. They had taken fifteen to twenty buses. The entire tribe sat together on one side, overlooking the road. I said to the

Dr. Pfau and her team investigate leprosy and tuberculosis cases in Neelam, a village in Azad Kashmir, Pakistan. The chances of survival of a poor mountain farmer, with his large family of three generations in a single cavelike room with no natural light, are not good, despite the support by the MALC team. Photo: DAHW, Hans Kutnewsky

boys, "What a wonderful opportunity. Here we have the whole tribe. What an excellent chance to begin your health education work."

"But how should we begin?" asked Jamal Khan. "If you come up with us they may take more notice of us."

I went with them and we bought oranges from one group. Jamal Khan introduced himself to the tribe. "And we have just come back from Karachi ..." Everyone gathered round and listened to the lads. The dialogue was in Pashto, which I could not understand. I could see now how Jamal Khan had grown. He climbed up onto a rock so that all could hear him. I joined him when he produced a needle. One of the tribesmen announced, "We are going to have our *jirga* (assembly of leaders). If you show me how to make a leprosy test then I shall be able to explain how to do it to the *jirga* members."

The two leprosy technicians showed how a test was made and the tribesmen watched intently. The road was made free and the boys had the great pleasure of knowing that the tribal elders had learned something from them. "We never realized that service could lead to *izzat* (honor)," said Jamal Khan to Kamran. "We had thought that *izzat* was only achieved by killing somebody, killing many people. If we had said that we had killed three enemies, another would say that he had killed six or seven or even eight. That's how we used to always measure *izzat*. But just by our leprosy work we were able to achieve *izzat* in the eyes of the whole tribe. Nobody before told us that service brought more *izzat* than *badla* (revenge)." To his revelation he added, "And when I take my place one day in the *jirga*, the son of our family enemy will probably also be in the *jirga*. I'll just tell him that I have decided to forget the past. And I bet he'll say then 'I'll forget, too.' And then there's a good chance that we will grow old together."

And so leprosy work is able to exert an influence on such complicated matters as the *vendetta*. I never discussed this problem explicitly with my boys. To give someone a built-in system of values and enlightenment through perception, this is our educational concept. That this is indeed happening always surprises and delights me anew.

7

Journeying Often

Just by Chance, in Yaghistan

It was the daily round, on tour somewhere in the north of Pakistan. It mostly poured rain in Yaghistan, especially in the Yalkot Valley, which was the first stop on our program. We knew that there was leprosy in the area but none of us had been there before. A patient had been to our outstation in January of that year. His son who accompanied him was diagnosed as an early case, too. We were able to diagnose five more early cases in the same family and we were informed about two more patients who lived farther up in the valley. We spent the night in the tiny stone house of a patient, five of us on three charpoys, together with three cows and our coughing leprosy patient, all in one dark, windowless room.

The next morning the whole village assembled. We set up our clinic on the flat roof of our patient's house. There was a flood of women, children, and men. Only Ibrahim could understand the language. The uproar, the icy wind whistling down from the mountains, and the sheer helplessness in the face of grinding poverty, all of this was heartrending and horrible. The condition of tiny Mussalin, who I had treated the day before for pneumonia, had now hopelessly worsened. I had sent one of his family members into the valley to fetch antibiotics (there was actually a "chemist" in the bazaar), but the medicines came too late.

A woman was in labor—she already had borne eight children. Only two had survived. Now the husband was telling me that I should do something so that she could give birth to a strong and healthy son. How could my iron tablets help her at this late stage, in her anemic condition? Perhaps for the next pregnancy.

The next four or five patients had no pathological findings: stomachache, pains in the limbs, backache. We gave out a handful of vitamin tablets. The next had a weak heart. We had some digitalis in the jeep and his son was asked to go down to the valley and fetch it. Next, please.

Dinner was ready at one—chapatis and some spicy vegetable stew. We were starving and extremely tired. But the stream of patients was seemingly endless. We decided to set out for the next village. Our leprosy patients were already waiting for us there.

As we began the descent the "please" and protests still echoed in our hearts. For the umpteenth time I was racking my brain to find a just solution to the problem of treating the many patients who sought help *and* to carry on further with the leprosy work. For years, this had been an unsolved problem. No, it is not the rock-strewn mountain paths nor the swaying suspension bridges high over surging rivers nor the nights spent in mountain huts, nor the scanty two meals a day that wear us down. It is this never-ending misery that we alone cannot alleviate. It is this that makes life so difficult.

Once, we were more than three thousand meters (almost two miles) high in a Himalayan village. A patient came running toward us. "My wife has just given birth but the afterbirth won't come out." I went immediately to the hut and at first could not make out what he meant. It was a poorly lit, cavelike room. Then it dawned on me. The woman had given birth to a daughter and had suffered a prolapse of the uterus. Her mother had assisted during delivery. Thinking that it was the afterbirth the poor woman had tried to remove the uterus completely. We had come by foot and had hardly anything with us. Anesthetic was out of question and there were no sterile instruments, but something had to be done immediately. I said, "If Mohammad Ali is not allowed inside I am not going to do a thing!" Finally, our leprosy technician was allowed inside the hut. I had only two aspirin and an unopened packet of Kleenex tissues with me—nothing more. At least the tissues were somewhat sterile. I washed my hands in a stream in front of the house and explained that I would have to do something on the spot because the woman would not survive the journey to the nearest hospital in her condition. The woman cooperated so bravely. During the operation we were all dripping with sweat. When the operation was over, we had to climb to some villages higher in the valley. Upon our return five days later, the woman was doing fine. I kept thinking, "We just came across this woman by chance. What on earth happens to the others?"

Sandstorm in the Desert

It was in 1971. We knew that there were leprosy patients in the desert area of Makran and that there were no treatment facilities available. None of us had been in this particular area before. It was also my first tour in a desert region. None of us was familiar with the route. At noon we set out for Jivani, the last outpost. We did not know, however, that there was a regular sandstorm in the afternoon hours.

Roads in the Pakistani hinterland are mostly dirt tracks. We simply followed the existing tracks left by previous vehicles. When the sand-storm hit us the tracks vanished. It was like driving in a dense fog. We were driving all over the place trying to find a break in the storm. Soon it was clear that we had lost our way. Then we ran out of fuel. We got out of the vehicle, the sand swirling around us, not knowing what we were going to do. Maybe we were just waiting for God to send a guardian angel to our rescue. Suddenly a dark shadow seemed to be coming straight at us. Slowly the shadow was transformed into a transport truck. We later learned that sometimes there is no vehicle on this track for up to eight days.

The truck driver got out to see what had happened. "Where do you want to go?"

"To Jivani."

"You'll never reach there."

"Okay, but can you show us the way?"

"You'll never find it. You'd better follow my rear light."

And we did exactly that. We drove on and on, always following the rear light. We were all afraid that one of us would run out of petrol, and the truck must have been short itself as they had given us some of their reserve. Suddenly the driver stopped. "The main road is over there!" he shouted. "When you come to some sand hills you're not far from Jivani." He turned around and drove on. We reached Jivani in the evening.

We toured the area for three weeks and found fifty-six untreated leprosy patients. One of them remains clearly in my mind. He was in a tiny, forgotten village by the coast. Our driver was a man who never missed his prayers. After prayers in the simple palm-roofed mosque he would call me and the examination of patients would begin. There was one case that looked bad but was curable. What shocked me deeply was the look the man gave me. It was the look of a terrified, hunted animal. I had thought that at least he would be happy at the news that he could be cured. Later on I learned about an eight-year-old boy, a leprosy patient, who was driven into this desert from that very village. That strange, haunted look now became more understandable.

> I love them because they are paving the way
> so that the downfallen and the suffering ones
> can obtain mercy. It is the joy of my life that
> through these workers I am able to help.

We had to do something. We subsequently have trained local leprosy technicians, men who are familiar with the terrain. If they have lost their way, these men can navigate by the stars or the position of the sun. They know the silent advent of the sandstorm and the time to venture into the desert. There is Ayub, there is Qasim, both touring Makran today. All of them are "my boys" and I love them because they are paving the way so that the downfallen and the suffering ones can obtain mercy. It is the joy of my life that through these workers I am able to help.

A Tribal Saga

Woe befalls the intruder foolish enough to trespass into the territory of an enemy tribe. The following incident happened during my second visit to a certain tribal area.

We were driving along a track that seemed to be leading in a straight line to nowhere, or so it appeared. All of a sudden we came to an abrupt breach in the road. From the vehicle we could only see the road seemingly continuing ahead; the dry riverbed could not be seen at all. We had to make a sudden turn, descend steeply, and then clamber up again. I held my breath. Safely at the other side, I said casually that I would report the matter to the authorities so that they could erect a warning sign. Why, after all, was there no such sign! "Well," the driver said, "we don't want one, and if anyone decided to erect one we would pull it down." To my inquiry whether any accidents had occurred he added, "Sure, jeeps do meet with accidents. But not ours. You see, it's a trap for intruders from other tribes. Only a few weeks back a car fell into it."

I was alarmed: "I hope nobody was hurt?"

"All four were killed," the driver said with satisfaction in his voice. "We know just where we have to turn off, the others don't." Such stories are typical. One can only imagine the problem a central government faces in such situations.

Kamran came from a tribal area that has not yet come under Pakistani jurisdiction. The area is still governed by tribal law—the law of the bullet. The honor of a man is judged by how he takes revenge on his enemies.

Kamran and his young friend, Jamal Khan, had completed their leprosy technician course in Karachi and I was traveling with them by jeep on their return journey to the tribal area. There was only one passable road, the rest were mountain paths only negotiable by foot. Kamran and Jamal Khan were in the backseat engaged in a heated discussion. Suddenly the conversation switched from the unintelligible Pashto to the more familiar Urdu. I was then brought into the conversation. "Something seems to have happened to my eyes in Karachi," said Kamran. "Could that be so, Doctor?"…"Or with our brain centers," said Jamal

Treatment at the side of the road in the desert region Makran, Balochistan. Photo: DAHW, Hans Kutnewsky

Khan, who had only recently been studying anatomy for his examination, "so that they are not quite in order?" I wanted to know what the problem was.

"Before," said Kamran, "when I used to go along the road I could see the rock ledge up there. It provided fantastic protection, and if an enemy came along it was quite easy to bump him off. Bang! Bang! But now I see women; women carrying water pitchers and heavy bundles of firewood. I suppose they must have been there before, but why didn't I see them? I think something must be wrong with my eyes."

"Or with our brain centers," retorted Jamal Khan.

"Or with your hearts?" I suggested.

Silence. Then a deep sigh. "Perhaps you're right," said Kamran.

Vendetta

In February 1980 we were in the north of Pakistan. The mountains were snowcapped. Winter sunshine streamed from a clear blue sky. The area of the left bank of the Indus River had only acceded to Pakistan a few years earlier. Before that, the inhabitants had been living according to their own laws, independent and closed off from the outside world. It was the law of the strongest, the law of the gun. In 1969, in the neighborhood of Pattan, we were besieged for two whole days by tribesmen from Yaghistan. They shot at anyone who dared to show himself in the bazaar area. The gorge is so narrow that one side of the river can be controlled from the opposite side. No house is without its watchtower, a slender edifice made from rough stones with a small opening toward the top, affording the occupant an excellent view of the valley and any approaching enemies, and a firm rifle support so that the aim can be more deadly. Every family has its vendetta. When one spends the night with someone, one has to explain the reason to the enemies of that household the following day. Hospitality is deeply engrained and carries a special significance. Before one can set foot in the village one must first ascertain which factions are in the vicinity, then the various groups are shared out. "We will have tea with you, and the evening meal with so-and-so's family. We'll spend the night with Yousuf and breakfast with Haleem." In this way, everyone is honored by a visit. In spite of such precautions there is still a lot of inquiry about where someone was seen and with whom.

The search for new leprosy cases in remote, difficult-to-access terrain is only possible with the support of local authorities. Here a tribal chief and religious leader in the region of Makran receives the survey team with Dr. Pfau, Father Daud, Mia-Kahn, and Sr. Jeannine for afternoon tea. For this special occasion women were permitted. Photo: DAHW, Hans Kutnewsky

One tour led us into the tribal mountain area. A merciless sun pierced the ravines, perilous paths wound ever upwards; there were near impassable glacial streams. Suddenly, the barking of a dog. Five paces farther on, there was an opening in the ravine and then a cluster of tiny stone houses, all perched on the edge of a precipice, with the watchtowers guarding the inhabitants of that mountain wilderness from possible enemy attack. Maize grew on the mountain terraces above. A woman separated herself from the small group of peasants in the midst of harvesting and ran toward us, her long dress and veil fluttering in the mountain breeze. She took me in both arms and kissed my hands in welcome. My walking stick was snatched away (she had nothing else to take; the technicians were carrying all the baggage). Before I could ask Abdullah who she was and also find out the meaning of such a greeting (because I had not met the woman before) she had ushered me into a one-room stone hut, damp and windowless. I could see nothing until my eyes became accustomed to the dark. Then gradually everything became as clear as it could in the smoky room.

A man, in his late thirties perhaps, sat up from where he was lying and stretched out his hands toward us. Deformed hands. A leprosy patient. He greeted Abdullah like a long-lost friend. His wife arranged cushions for us on the mat and brought us goat milk. She looked imploringly at me, and then said something in Sheena, which I could not understand. Abdullah translated: "She says the boy is still in jail. *He* is out on bail, because he has got leprosy." And this is the story.

Mohammad Akram had a sister; she was fair, blue-eyed, with long jet-black plaits. The village lads used to crane their necks as she went on her way to the well in the early morning hours. Two tribal elders were demanding her hand in marriage to form a union, which would solve an old vendetta. Mohammad Akram had been hesitating over the decision for a long time now. Then, suddenly, one day he decided on one of the suitors. "I couldn't give the girl to both of them, neither could I keep her at home. But on the wedding night the rival faction attacked. As I had been forewarned, I had placed my eldest son on guard in the watchtower. The first bullet struck a tribal elder. What else could I do? I had to defend my family. There has been enmity between our families for a long time, the usual vendettas."

The death penalty was warranted by Pakistani law. Mohammad Akram and his son were handed over to the police and put in jail. The sentence for murder was death by hanging. This meant that the family would be left in the village unprotected. Only the ancient grandfather was in the house, and he had such an advanced case of leprosy that he could barely crawl along on hands and knees. Who would protect the women from sudden attack? Mohammad Akram continued the story.

"I racked my brain to find out how I could get out of prison. Finally, my sickness came to my aid. I presented a report on my disease to the prison superintendent. He was so terrified of leprosy that he made an application for me to be released on bail that very day."

Mohammad Akram could not leave his place of asylum. If any of the enemy camp came across him he was a sitting duck. But he kept a rifle ready by his side in order to protect his family.

"And the boy is *still* in jail," the mother said, sadly.

Silence. A hopeless, heavy silence hung in the air. The grandfather crawled around the room and then sat huddled by the door. There was a pair of earthenware vessels, an old goatskin used for carrying water, and a gun hanging on the wall. Nothing else was in the room.

These were people imprisoned by tribal law and no one knew how to break out of it. "Then?" I said to Abdullah.

"Have the boy declared a leprosy patient," he said gloomily. "What else is left?"

"But the vendetta?" I asked.

"That will go on according to the rules. When the other side announces that Mohammad Akram is on the list, there can be no escape."

"Then is there no solution?" I asked.

"Blood money," Abdullah said. "That is, if the other side agrees. But who is going to pay it?" "Ask Akram," I said. "Should his children all die on the gallows because this vendetta *must* be carried out to the last letter?"

Blood money. And again the conversation was drowned in waves of Sheena. Aslam muttered away in monosyllables. His wife brought hot maize bread and tea. Abdullah said that even if he sold everything, including land and cows, there still would not be enough to pay the blood money.

"How much does he actually need?" I asked.

"About eight thousand rupees," Abdullah replied.

"And then?" I wondered.

"He could go and work as a day laborer in Gilgit. I can arrange this."

"And the family?" I asked.

"He can take them with him."

"And is this blood money able to settle everything?" I queried.

"Yes," Abdullah said. "According to tribal law, everything."

We chewed on chapatis and sipped hot tea. We tried to look at the consequences of selling the land of one's forefathers. What did the grandfather say about this? But it meant the boy would be released from jail and the murder charges withdrawn. The mother gave us an imploring look.

Outside, Akram's youngest child was chasing some squawking chickens. A few sunbeams slanted through an opening in the roof and into the darkened room. The grandfather sighed. He was saying something. "What use are the fields to the children," translated Abdullah, "when they will die on the gallows because the vendetta *must* be carried out?"

On the return journey through the ravine, I asked Abdullah, "Are you sure that you can find work for them?"

"Yes," he replied.

"And will you be able to raise the eight thousand rupees?" This question was addressed to me. The answer was in the affirmative. "The lives of seven people, 1,150 rupees per person," I said.

I took a deep breath and shut my eyes. In front of me the face of the wife, the eyes of a mother, blossomed with hope. "The boy, they won't hang him, will they? They'll let him free, won't they?"

"Are you all right?" asked Abdullah, concerned.

"Sure," I said, clambering down the rocky path. "I am just happy."

Women's Woes

There are some tribes in which the condition of women is enough to make the very heavens weep. That it is not perceived as discrimination is no excuse and in no way removes the degradation. For me, it is a discrimination that cuts deeply and makes my blood boil. When dinner is brought in, it is the men who are served first; the leftovers are sent back to the women's quarters. One should see *how* the men eat in this part of Pakistan! Because I am a foreigner, I am as privileged as a man. Nevertheless, if I could live a second life I would certainly dedicate myself full time to women's rights in Pakistan!

Mostly a woman's function is to bear children—male children, of course. Her value is judged according to the number of *sons* she is able to bear. When a man is asked how many children he has, the answer is given in sons. In the countryside, a woman is just a source of unpaid labor. The men make her life more miserable because of their never-ending vendettas, blood feuds that are male-made and carried out to their gruesome conclusions by males only. Many of the men have more than one wife. During a stay in one of these villages in the north we were guests of a village elder who was about fifty-seven years old. He had four wives. When introducing himself he announced in a quite disgusting way that none of these women was able to bear him a child. How I regretted not being able to speak Sheena, the local language! Then I could have told that fellow, in front of his wives, "When *you* are impotent you cannot put blame on the women!" So I could only advise through a translator, "Go off to the nearest government clinic and get yourself a semen test."

We climbed five kilometers (about three miles) up a mountain, following a patient's daughter. She was the second wife of a peasant and had a bone tumor on the frontal cavity. Her face was swollen and deformed. It really looked frightful. But instead of taking the poor woman to a hospital, her husband simply remarried. She was still good enough to milk the cows and work in the fields. I could have strangled the man in cold blood! In the evening, we reached a mountain hut, shivering and exhausted from the climb. Abdullah spoke with the peasants who were delighted with our visit and brought out two charpoys. A woman busied herself with the bed linen. She put a cover on the ground for me to sit on. Before I could make a move some men had occupied the place.

The social position of women also has repercussions on our work. We are only able to reach two-thirds of the population because our workers are not allowed to examine female patients. As a rule, the local girls are not allowed to join an all-male team. We cannot send a married couple out into the field either because any leprosy technician who makes his wife work would lose his social prestige. This then interferes with his community acceptance and thus the efficiency of his work. The only solution is to bring in foreign female workers. But then there are visa restrictions and rules that prevent foreigners from setting foot in at least two-thirds of Pakistani territory affected by leprosy. I am getting on in years and often wonder what will happen when I retire. The government of Azad Kashmir bends over backward to assist me, however, a visiting permit for another female worker cannot be granted. Why? It cannot be done because it cannot be done. So we use every imaginable trick to try to get around the problem. Even to the extent of having the boys grow beards to appear older and therefore more respectable in the eyes of the community. In this way they can at least examine the visible parts of a woman. We gave the oldest woman in one village daily wages so that she could escort the boys and spread the news in the women's quarters to at least find out if anyone had any whitish or reddish patches. Her job was to convince the women that it was only the patch that the boys were interested in and to persuade anyone with such a symptom to come forward for treatment. With all these contrivances, we are nevertheless slowly making headway.

The subordination of the female sex does not have any roots in the Holy Qur'an. It is the product of tribal structures. Leprosy work cannot be successful in the long run without raising the consciousness of the people.

Success in Salwar Kameez

I was with a group of five traveling in a Land Rover through the desert area of Makran. Somehow nothing seemed to work out well. Whenever we approached a group of tents, the women would run for their lives, children under their arms, the older children running behind them, screaming.

We held a council of war. Daud, the local leprosy technician, came up with a likely explanation. "Your Punjabi-style salwar kameez looks

A remote meeting place for people without modern telecommunications at the interface of two side valleys of the Neelum Valley in Pakistan-administered Kashmir. When the word spread that the German doctor was going to be there, seriously ill women, men, and children waited since dawn in the hope of being treated. Photo: DAHW, Hans Kutnewsky

like a man's outfit in their eyes, and perhaps from a distance the women can't identify you." The argument seemed convincing. We managed to get a Makrani costume with wide baggy breeches and a long, multicolored, loose-fitting dress—so loose that if one were expecting twins, that fact could be hidden from everybody. Then came a veil to cap it all. The result was amazing. When we approached any group of tents, the women came milling around us. We parked our ambulance by the tents and sat on a charpoy, placed under the friendly shade of a date palm. The news of our arrival spread like wildfire. The sick came from near and far. I sat on the captain's deck (the charpoy) and gave directions to the team: "First do the leprosy examination, take temperature and blood pressure over there—that woman!" I had completely forgotten that I was wearing Makrani clothes. Out in the field the local leprosy technician gave the orders; on the journey the driver was the leader, and now, during the consultation I was in command. All seemed to be going as planned. Then the penetrating, observing, and delighted scrutiny of two young girls pulled me out of my role. They were sitting on the ground propped up against the tent pegs, tittering behind their veils and enjoying this totally new situation with large, amused eyes. Someone dressed just like them was sitting on the captain's deck and commanding this pack of men!

Arising consciousness? Perhaps not. But, in a way, it was a lesson with a touch of humor. So it probably will be forgotten.

8

Reflections By the Wayside

Along the Wayside

What keeps me going are the happenings along the wayside. There is a road leading to Astore that is so suicidal and dangerous that even seasoned drivers have to dope themselves before negotiating it. But there is no other road. The journey up was not too bad because we did not know what lay ahead. Our mission was over and we had to go back. I am able to sleep under most conditions. On this dark night, however, I was only able to wonder how we were going to get out of this place in one piece.

It was May 13. We had twenty kilometers (about 12½ miles) more to go and we trembled every inch of the way. During the night there had been slight rain. As we set out we noticed that a jeep had gone before us. We could follow its tracks in the mud and could judge the width of the road ahead. At least it was wide enough for the vehicle to have made it in one piece. For the whole twenty kilometers I just stared at the tire tracks and thought, "Well, he's made it."

Then we came around a corner and saw the suspension bridge in front of us and the narrow ravine through which the wind howled unceasingly. The bridge was swaying to the sound of the wind, and we had to wait for the right moment so that the vehicle could be steered gently onto it, the weight stopping the swaying. Safely on the other side, the adventure came to an end.

Where do I get authority to expose the entire team again and again and again to these dangers?

Somewhere in our Holy Books, Jesus of Nazareth, this prophet for the Muslims and this revelation of God for the Christians, says, "I am the way and follow me. I have done it; you will make it, too. The jeep got through; you will get through, too. Because it's me who sends you on the mission, don't be afraid."

Lesson by the Indus

Shortly after a trade union crisis, which nearly succeeded in bringing me to the end of my tether, I was on tour along the Indus River on the way to Skardu. When the snow thaws, the Indus becomes a most unattractive muddy flood. When the water level begins to drop, some of the water remains in depressions in the rocks, forming small lakes. Because all connection with the river is lost, the silt sinks to the bottom and the color changes into an unbelievable azure blue.

Immersed in admiring this phenomenon of nature, this crystal clear blue image of heaven, I thought, that is the answer. Withdraw from the world and life will be like these miniature lakes: peaceful, serene, and beautiful.

> Somewhere in our Holy Books, Jesus of Nazareth, this prophet for the Muslims and this revelation of God for the Christians, says, "I am the way and follow me. I have done it; you will make it, too. The jeep got through; you will get through, too. Because it's me who sends you on the mission, don't be afraid."

But on my return journey I saw that the lakes were drying up and the thought struck me: withdrawing from the hurts of life would be just like this; in a few months, I would be all dried up.

Being hurled about like a cork in a raging torrent is a part of life. To soil your hands is unavoidable. The alternative may be pleasantly eccentric but definitely unsuitable. I shall be eternally grateful to the Indus for giving me this insight.

Living Water

Water, living water. For us in Pakistan it is indeed living water. Water, which begets life. Whenever I fly to Islamabad, I keep an eye out for the desert of Sindh. Then suddenly the Indus comes into sight and the desert is replaced by green. One cannot help but hold one's breath seeing how that living water has awakened everything into life. Parts of the Indus look like an ugly, slimy brew but, in spite of this, life blooms around it. And for the umpteenth time I think, why have you not yet learned the lesson, even if the water is dirty? How often does it only take just a bit of dirty water and life flourishes again!

> Being hurled about like a cork in a raging torrent is a part of life. To soil your hands is unavoidable. The alternative may be pleasantly eccentric but definitely unsuitable.

The Indus can be fascinating. From its source in the trans-Himalayan Ladakh ranges of western Tibet it makes its headlong journey through Pakistan on its way to the warm waters of the Arabian Sea. Piercing a way through the rocky mountains of the Northern Districts, it forms a gigantic, hundreds-of-kilometers-long gorge. This part of the Indus has always disappointed and frustrated me—a rocky desert almost devoid of vegetation. Any silt washed ashore is taken away by the torrents born from the melting snow. In this area the water cannot be harnessed and the Indus is totally useless for those living along its bank. But in the glacial area, high up in the mountains, there is a wonderful belt of green with flowers and life around the glacial lakes, fed by tiny little rivulets that never manage to reach the thundering river in the gorge. They just disappear in the gravel and clefts on their rocky descent. Life admits futility.

At every turn I come across such thought-provoking experiences in Pakistan.

Rider on the White Horse

Death has always fascinated me. Perhaps I sometimes think death is "returning." I cannot see death as the traditional mower, an old bearded man with a scythe. My "death" is a rider, the "Rider on the White Horse." This imagery stems from my eschatological belief, an image of my Holy Books. I imagine myself standing on a hill and running down to meet him. This imagery also plays a role in my readiness to face death—I am fascinated by death, not by dying. In death, however, I have the image of myself falling into the arms of someone for whose tender embrace I have shed a lifetime of tears. Did my attitude toward death develop out of the many perilous situations of my life? I do not know. For two years

I lived under the threat of an erroneous medical diagnosis or, to be more exact, a diagnosis that did not come to the predicted conclusion. I was living under the impression that these would be the last two years of my life, yet they were some of the happiest and most beautiful years I have lived. At that time I was in the north and it seemed as if it would be my last journey. I lost myself in the glory of the vines clinging to the walnut trees; in light and warmth and color. Something so precious, perishable, like a transparency of things to come. If God made the world already so breathtakingly beautiful, what then will the beatific vision be like!

What Do We Have in Common?

Islam and Christianity: two monotheistic religions, each of them confesses truth as a central mystery of their faith. Revealed truth, truth received through God's free bounty, his precious gift carried in exquisitely fragile vessels and placed in our hands. Entrusted to our hearts. Revealed truth, which we simply cannot betray.

Is it possible for two religions, each claiming to confess eternal truth, to engage in any meaningful dialogue? I have no answer to this question. I can relate only living experiences, the experiences of one in search of eternal truth, and being able to recognize a fellow seeker on the way even though the road may differ from the one chalked out for him. It is the common search for a common eternal home that binds us together in brotherhood, in sisterhood.

> It is the common search for a common eternal home that binds us together in brotherhood, in sisterhood.... My hope is that we can learn to live our dialogue in love and concern for the other without betraying the eternal truth entrusted to us by revelation. Living our lives spelling out this truth, giving our lives confessing this truth.

My hope is that we can learn to live our dialogue in love and concern for the other without betraying the eternal truth entrusted to us by revelation. Living our lives spelling out this truth, giving our lives confessing this truth, even if sacrifices are asked from us every day.

On a less intellectual level, how would this dialogue be carried on between those of us who are engaged in a common mission? Most of it is just life, lived truth, shining through our actions. Sometimes, however, it becomes thematic.

Gul Hasan has come into contact with a Tabligh group. I can see day by day how his life is changing, to the point of even questioning such sacred values as *izzat* and the blood feud. I pray hard for the boy that he may persevere, backing him up with a rare patience when he delays the team once more because of his numerous prayer sessions. There are many occasions when he makes an observation and I nod my approval, or I make a statement and he agrees with the freshness of his new discovery, which makes old truths shine afresh for me as well. We discover day by day how much we have in common.

One evening, the group wanted to know what I actually believed in. For a moment I was at a loss to explain. They knew how I lived. I have never put the *why* into English or Urdu. I would hardly have been able to supply a ready formula in German. Love is love. Who can explain it? But the group wanted an answer. Once more I groped for words to define the inexpressible.

Love is love. Who can explain it?

"God," I said, "because he is *God*, is so infinite and so much above our tiny human understanding that we could never know anything about him, except vaguely suspecting something divine behind flowers and children and mountain streams. In life and love and death. So that we could know more about God he had to reveal himself in some comprehensible way.

"As I understand it, Muslims believe that God chose Muhammad (peace be upon him) and revealed the Holy Qur'an to him. God came in the form of this Holy Book. The Holy Qur'an is the Word of God. The Prophet Muhammad (peace be upon him) is the perfect human, an example for all to emulate.

"As a Christian, I believe that God became incarnate in the form of Jesus of Nazareth. I believe that he revealed himself as the Logos, the Word. I believe that the scriptures record his message and the events in his life. I believe that he lived on earth, with men, so that we in turn could come to know how to live our lives. That he was a carpenter—just that, a carpenter—as if to prove how precious our tiny, insignificant lives are and how much God loves us.

"Let me just try to relate it to our work," I continued, "something about leprosy control.

"There are two ways of teaching the new multidrug therapy. A manual is compiled. You read it, your senior leprosy workers explain it to you, and you organize the work according to the directions in the manual.

"The other way is to ask someone to accompany you in the field to do the work with you. To live your lives. And while you are observing that person you are able to learn how to administer the multidrug therapy yourselves.

"God wants to teach man, whom he himself has created, to walk in his truth. For Muslims, I think, it is the 'Manual' that is important, the Manual with its divine and crystal clear message. Christians believe in emulating the example of Jesus, following in his footsteps. For Muslims, God's Word is mysteriously present in his Holy Book. For us Christians he is present in the life and love and sacrifice of this Joshua of Nazareth, this Jesus. But, I believe that both ways lead us on the way to the one holy and immortal God." The group listened pensively. Later on, they will come back to it.

> I believe that it helps us to overcome animosity, brings us closer together so that we learn to accept one another, not in spite of, not because of, but in this otherness. I believe that this otherness enriches us, and that any such work for peace is simultaneously work for God—because God is peace, because God is love and wants us to live in peace and love.

How can our common work and mission lead us to Muslim-Christian dialogue? I believe that it helps us to overcome animosity, brings us closer together so that we learn to accept one another, not in spite of, not because of, but in this otherness. I believe that this otherness enriches us, and that any such work for peace is simultaneously work for God—because God is peace, because God is love and wants us to live in peace and love.

"Interreligious dialogue deepens our awareness of the treasures of our own religion while opening our hearts to the experience that God is incomprehensible, that his love is without bounds." —Dr. Ruth Pfau

Dialogue between people who know, love, and accept one another, done in deference to each other, deepens our faith, our own spiritual commitment. Interreligious dialogue is not meant to blur or obscure the truth for which we stand, to destroy revealed truth of which we are the caretakers. Interreligious dialogue deepens our awareness of the treasures of our own religion while opening our hearts to the experience that God is incomprehensible, that his love is without bounds, that he has created every man in his likeness, that he is the Master of the present, the past, and the future, and that he wants us to be perfect, "even as he is perfect."

Trees Without Leaves

In 1968 I revisited Germany for the first time after eight years. I was able to meet Samuel and Rafiq, two leprosy workers who were doing their nursing training there. Rafiq told me his first impressions of Germany when he had arrived three years earlier: "The trees were so bare, just like sticks in the ground. I used to wait for the leaves to come out and when they didn't and didn't come, I told Samuel that German trees don't have any leaves." Now when anyone makes some sweeping generalization or rash judgment on the developing world, Rafiq, Samuel, and I say, "Oh, yes … and German trees don't have any leaves."

Whenever I am in Germany I always come across the opinion that Pakistan is a militant, undemocratic, Islamic dictatorship. It only hits the headlines because of rights violations. During the decades I have had the opportunity to study this developing country on site, so to speak. I have visited every single corner of the country. Of course there are problems. It took a long time before even I was able to give up generalizing. But when one is able to see things with one's own eyes and subsequently through the eyes of the other, everything takes on a different complexion.

I am reproached with "Oh, but they have the death penalty in Pakistan." I told some people of a case that I had encountered. A father had killed his own daughter with an axe because she had a liaison with a young chap from the village. The parents of the unfortunate couple sentenced both of them to death. The boy was shot dead by his father and the girl was axed to death by her father. It is probably difficult to imagine such a thing taking place: the father with an axe, the girl screaming. In another place, a crowd stoned a mother and daughter to death. In a country where self-justice is administered so easily, one cannot judge the death penalty sentenced by the courts by European standards.

On the other hand, since I am increasingly engaged in human rights cases, I am sick, *sick,* of what is going on in Pakistan, and not only in Pakistan. Domestic violence. Police violence. Daily violence in the streets, in the neighborhoods. Suicide attacks. Wherever did we go wrong? What should I do? Go home? Or try—whenever it comes my way—to do something, a little thing, whenever such a case crosses my path? Our way? Sit in police lock-up to keep the interrogation, the treatment of the suspect, human? Pay lawyer bills, bail money for people without resources? Visit people in jail to let them feel that somewhere somebody did not forget them? Network with the many brave initiatives in Pakistan and abroad?

What can we do? What can we all do?

Surely watch out for the tiny unnecessary hurts we cause others during our day. Join one of the groups who try not to let this suffering be forgotten by us, the more fortunate ones. Lend our voice to the voiceless.

PART II

9

Working for Peace under Wartime Conditions

D-day through the Night in a Burka

Summer 1984, D-day. Shall we get over the border? It is the middle of the night, about 3 a.m. We are departing from Quetta. I slip secretly into a burka, which is the full-body veil of the Muslim woman, and steal out of the monastery of the Saint Joseph Sisters who have put me up for the past few days. I told them that I was going, as usual, on outpatient service. I did not want to get them tied up in our illegal adventure.

A red Toyota Landcruiser rides off with the leader of the rebels. Haji is at the wheel. I am in a yellow-gold burka next to him and Hassan is in the backseat. The barrier at the edge of the city opens as if by itself. Either they know the red jeep or someone slipped the guard something.

The security precautions around Quetta are very strict. At this crossing barrier, I always have to get out and empty the Toyota for the border guards. The night is pitch black. Five kilometers (about three miles) away from the edge of the city we stop and get out. Our eyes have adjusted to the darkness. We can make out the outline of a fully packed Toyota exactly the same as our own, which is parked on the city edge.

We change cars. The red jeep, with Haji driving, turns and is lost in the darkness. Hardly two sentences of Persian have been exchanged.

I do not know either of the men in this second Toyota jeep. One of them speaks English. It is good that Hassan is next to me otherwise I would feel entirely lost.

Was I upset or excited? I do not know now. I only remember that it was crazily adventuresome and the fulfillment of an old dream.

Through the Steppes of Balochistan

An endless trip through Balochistan. We come to a military strip and the road is well guarded. I go undercover. The tent-shaped burka veils me completely. There is only a tiny flap. I can see through the burka but it does not reveal whoever is hidden beneath it. The men in the jeep, though they are Afghanis, have Pakistani passports.

The road consists of tire tracks in the desolate infinity of the prairie-desert. We are thirsty, exhausted, encrusted with dust. We are too tired in the jeep even to read something in order to kill the boring uniformity of the hours. I pray my rosary. Then I think of Hamid. Hamid is one of the first leprosy technicians from Balochistan. Currently he is responsible for running our program in the entire province. He is the provincial leprosy field officer, a midcareer position. It is a position that has done a great deal of good for our project.

How often have I traveled this route! Not to Afghanistan, but in search of leprosy patients in the border area in Balochistan.

> Was I upset or excited? I do not know now. I
> only remember that it was crazily adventuresome
> and the fulfillment of an old dream.

Badmi. Farther through the desolate prairie-desert, on an endless road, after twelve hours of travel through dust and heat, around 3 p.m., Badmi is finally in sight. It is a dreary gathering of mud huts in a bleak prairie area. It is the Pakistani border station of the mujahideen but it already has more the feel of Afghanistan than Pakistan.

I have memories of the mujahideen group of friends, which Hassan had put together in exile at this border post in Badmi. The leader of this group was my first contact with the resistance back then, in Rawalpindi.

I remember it all exactly. One night in Rawalpindi, a jeep stopped at our staff house. Two bearded men emerged. They spoke neither Urdu nor English. The resistance fighters said they could bring grain, blankets, and shoes to central Afghanistan if we had the necessary money to help them. Hassan translated it all. I promised to do my best. They had already brought a European group of medical staff across the so-called gray border. Later, we met again at irregular intervals and slowly the plan of this first expedition took shape.

Flood Danger

In Badmi, we are welcomed. They share unleavened bread and tea with us. I am still enclosed in my burka and fall asleep dead tired in the back of the jeep.

At 3 a.m., we make a hasty departure to go farther on the road toward Afghanistan. It is a moonless, starless night. It begins to rain. We have been mysteriously warned about that. How? By the drumming in the bush, the language of which I only learn to interpret later.

Rain in this region means the possibility of a dangerous flood. Sand transforms itself into treacherous mud. So our driver decides on an immediate takeoff. He is the one with the responsibility. If you wait too long and the water sinks into the ground, then you sink into the morass and are lost.

The sand dunes at the side of the riverbed have already transformed themselves into deep mud. No wonder that we are stuck here. The tires get stuck more deeply with every attempt to turn them. Five of us are in the car, two young resistance fighters, the driver, Hassan, and me. We are in the middle of the desert in complete darkness.

Suddenly the four men jump out of the car and disappear into the night. I have no idea where they have gone. Presumably, they are seeking the fort. I sit in the car, listening anxiously, holding my breath, waiting and waiting, until doing nothing is simply intolerable to me. So I open the doors of the jeep. Perhaps I will be able to hear something. Or should I call the men? I attempt to get out and am already sunk knee-deep into the morass. I make a quick retreat to the secure seat in the jeep and I listen again in the night.

Then Hassan emerges, along with Ibrahim, Ashraf, and Jan Ali. Ibrahim jumps in the driver's seat and starts the engine, and the others push the jeep. When they are all sitting in the car again, they are spattered from head to toe. The jeep fights its way through the muck, but it manages to do it. After five minutes we are once again secure, out on a rocky surface. It is a surface of prairie, with little thorny bushes. The road, which only has tire tracks, is ahead of us in the faded appearance of the blinding headlights.

Poppies in the Bomb Crater

There is actually no proper border in a strict sense between Pakistan and Afghanistan. In the north there are the mountain tribes, which are at home on both sides of the so-called official border.

I had been in Afghanistan once before. Back then I did not even know it. Members of mountain tribes refuse to answer when they are asked, "Do we find ourselves now in Pakistan or are we still in Afghanistan?" For them, this border does not exist. In 1947, when the division of the Indian subcontinent into India and Pakistan took place, there was no officially negotiated and settled northern border. So this border is unnatural culturally, insofar as members of the same mountain tribe live on both sides.

Only a few sections of the border are guarded whereas at the Khyber Pass you must always pass a border station. It is different in the tribal area. They have nomadic Afghanis who always come to certain meadows in Pakistan, stay there during the winter, and then go back to Afghanistan.

The rain has stopped now. In the gray of the morning, the first Afghani sentry is visible. We have more long hours of travel through desolate prairie mountain passages without vegetation, through narrow valleys and wide expanses.

Later, we come upon an agriculturally productive area. Life here seems so normal and peaceful. The farmers till their fields. Goat shepherds feed their herds. For hours, we can completely forget that we are in a war zone—until we travel through that first bombed-out village and see abandoned fields overgrown with weeds and scorched earth, a legacy of the war policy of the central government. Blood-red poppies are blooming in a bomb crater.

Years later, in 1987, when I traveled again through the same village, a child sat on the ruins and two fields were sown. So life goes on.

Hassan Returns

Hassan gives us some figures. The resident population of Afghanistan is seventeen million. Three to four million have fled to Pakistan, about half as many to Iran. Perhaps a million people have managed to make it to the West. Another million have been killed in battle. It is all tragic because Afghanistan needs every one of its people.

What makes me happy—and also a little bit proud—is that Hassan, a former leprosy patient and our current leprosy assistant, who had been able to lead a secure and well-ordered life in Karachi, has now come back in order to help his countrymen. What awaits him is a wearying jeep trip every day, a life of constant scarcity and danger, and the burdensome responsibility for an area shaken by tribal rivalries and threatened from without. In ten weeks I will be going back to Pakistan and then he has to stand through it all himself. So this is the moment of birth for the leprosy control program in Afghanistan.

For three years Hassan was the translator for all the Afghani patients in our hospital in Karachi. The misery was not abstract for him. It was not a matter of numbers. For three years he heard the suffering of families in their homes. He saw the horror in the faces of people. We had, in the meantime, almost forgotten how horrible leprosy can be if it is not treated in time. We were only able to show many complications of this illness during the training period in our slide transparencies. Now we have them again—live!—in the wards.

Suddenly the leprosy station was once again full of crippled, blind human beings all covered with wounds. And this was only the tip of the iceberg. What really shocked us was that very seldom was there a woman among them. Obviously the men had succeeded in getting across this unguarded border and through the desert and prairie area, but the women suffering from leprosy had not made it across alive.

Once again it was a matter of the weakest in the social hierarchy being hit. If you wanted to help them, you had to seek them out yourself.

Back then, it was clear to me that our chances for fighting leprosy were better in Afghanistan than in Pakistan because we could begin with an experienced core group. In 1983, Hassan and Mubarik did exploratory work in the area from which most of our leprosy patients came, in order to find out whether a treatment center was possible there at all. I had promised to come along if they saw any sense in it. After their return, the light turned green.

Welcome to Afghanistan

So now we are in Afghanistan. It is 6 p.m. Before us is the Kandahar-Kabul "highway" guarded by a Russian sentry. The post has radar devices and rocket throwers. We travel in broad daylight toward the road.

"It's unlikely that they'll shoot," says Hassan.

"Why?" I want to know.

"Because they are scared of the revenge measures conducted by the mujahideen if they shoot one of our vehicles."

It is twenty minutes later, the post and the road lie behind us now. We are out of the range of the rockets, in an area that lies firmly in the hands of the rebels. I have dreamed of this moment since 1969.

Late evening. It is pitch-dark. We have been on the way for twenty-three hours, nonstop. The jeep takes a sharp turn, follows a steeply rising path, and then stops. A door opens. Lanterns shine. Somebody says in fluent English, "Welcome." One minute later, we are relaxing on colorful mattresses that have been put down for us in the guest room. We have tea.

When I close my eyes, I am still in the jeep. When I open them, the room begins to swirl around me. The driver is in a great mood.

"The most beautiful drive that I've had since the war broke out," he says. "No difficulties! Boy, did we have a great time!" We laugh at Hassan's stories, told in Persian, which I cannot even follow.

I am dead tired. I have already fallen asleep before the food is served.

10

Afghanistan—My Dream, My Nightmare

My Conference with the President

I am occupying a position of a national cabinet officer in Pakistan, where such officials are professional civil servants. For that reason, they ordinarily survive changes of government, because they are the experts most difficult to replace. Even when I work on an honorary basis, it is still an official position.

The president had already done a great deal for leprosy work, so it would have been unfair to keep our Afghanistan plans secret from him. And if someone had caught me, then anyone could say, "You see, this general sent his female spy, under the cover of Christian charity, into the area of the rebellion."

I sought the president's permission to launch a leprosy program in Afghanistan, but what would happen if the president had said no? Understandably I was nervous. I began the conference quite diplomatically. "With the coming of the refugees, we are receiving an entirely new wave of leprosy patients into the country."

The president said he knew that and asked, "Do you have an idea?"

"Yes," I said, "One has to catch the leprosy wave in Afghanistan. Every healed person who returns sends us five new cases."

He understood that we had to fight the problem at the source, in Afghanistan.

"Any kind of concrete plan?" he wanted to know.

"Yes," I said.

Silence.

"Do you want to go yourself?" he asked.

"Yes," I said.

I see him still, how he sat, leaned back in his chair. When I said yes, he jumped up, clapped his hands, and said, "Wonderful!"

It also was the president who placed the Toyota Landcruiser at our disposal.

Into My Land of Dreams—Illegally

In 1984, for the first time, I went illegally into Afghanistan, which at that time was torn apart by the nightmare of the war. Hassan and Mubarik, the two Afghani leprosy assistants on our Karachi team, were the moving force. They wanted to go back to their country when Mumtaz, a twenty-three-year-old refugee from their homeland, almost died in their hands from complications caused by untreated leprosy. They really did go back, and then Hassan returned and said, "It's possible, you can work there." Naturally, there was a great deal of adventure associated with this suggestion, but it was not just that. We had also observed a great deal of need there.

A difficult climb in rough terrain to get to patients. Photo: Prof. Martin Gertler

Afghanistan had always been my dream. I did not want to die without having worked in Azad Kashmir. The high place of Hazarajat was another dream. In 1984, as I finally stood in Hazarajat, I thought, in the list of my childhood dreams, the only things still missing are Tibet and the moon.

Hazarajat, an alien rock-desert, is enveloped in violet twilight in the evening light. It is a prairie area with a few thorny bushes. Occasionally, quite unexpectedly, there is a small river and then a valley opens up that is of a special green because it has been so long since one has seen green.

And then this limitless expanse. The Afghani highlands produce the impression that you only have to jump and you would be able to fly. This land is a runway takeoff into eternity.

How the Afghani boys ride their horses without saddles! The riders melt into the animals. When I sit on a horse, I sit on a horse. But one discovers the art of riding when one has seen those Afghani boys.

And the courage of those people who stay and survive in this country, their indomitable will to survive! Somewhere in the mountains is a tiny water source that is rechanneled with endless patience, perseverance, and an indomitable wealth of inventiveness. Tiny fields are sowed in the hope that, sometime or another, it will rain. At harvest time, every single ear of corn will be picked in these highlands, just as we pick bouquets of flowers. Every blade of grass will be harvested and dried out for animals to eat. Whatever is left of the low thorn bushes will be carefully gathered for heating in the winter and for cooking meals.

Already in the 1960s, the Afghani government, at that time still under the king, had asked us whether we would be willing to train Afghani leprosy assistants. At that time our staff still did not have anyone who spoke the Persian language. And I did not know then how everything was supposed to start and continue in Pakistan.

Nonetheless, the dream of starting a leprosy program in Afghanistan remained.

And then came the outpatient station in Malistan, which we opened. It survived. So Hassan and Mubarik continued to work.

And I dreamed, dreamed, dreamed that I would one day return to Afghanistan and help the staff build the network of treatment centers. And I did return.

Who Loves the People?

What did this time in my life mean for me?

In Afghanistan I almost went crazy because of the unimaginable suffering. I once stood before a six-year-old who was suffering from a kidney stone, which causes the most terrible pain that a human being can endure. We did not have any means for operating on him. The screams of this boy when he was suffering outbreaks of colic follow me still today.

How did I cope with all this as a Christian? I did not cope. I put this case on my eschatological list and will be asking Him, "Why did you permit this, You, who love this six-year-old boy even more than I could?"

I could not help the boy. I could only assure the mother, with tears in my eyes, that I felt the same way as she did.

Or the twenty-year-old man who had been injured in underground resistance warfare and died because we could not perform blood transfusions. He died as helicopters flew over us that would have been able to take him to a hospital in Kabul in twenty minutes.

All that is so absurd and so meaningless.

Yet there is this impossible-to-believe, irrational, atrocious, overwhelming mystery (which Christians of all walks of life have been believing over two thousand years): it is said that it is God—God—who identifies himself with those who suffer.

> Somewhere in our Holy Books it is written about Jesus ... that he loved them, and he loved them *to the very end*. Through suffering and mediocrity and betrayal and cowardice, he loved them. To the very end. That is the message, which again and again overcomes me. It is the message that makes it possible to go on, to keep hoping, to keep helping.

Somewhere in our Holy Books it is written about Jesus—this fascinating, incomprehensible carpenter from Palestine—that he loved them, and he loved them *to the very end*. Through suffering and mediocrity and betrayal and cowardice, he loved them. To the very end.

That is the message, which again and again overcomes me. It is the message that makes it possible to go on, to keep hoping, to keep helping. It is a message that gives us a glimpse, a fleeting glimpse, that there will be an answer, somewhere, somehow, sometime, at a moment of freedom, when we are delivered from our preconditioned views, our so-called reality. The moment I am longing for.

Maybe this hope, which will not die, enables me to live much more consciously the "small goodbyes" that are practice sessions for the great parting.

> Love, limitations, illness, and death are the
> fundamental experiences of human existence.
> Love and death: they are life, and life hurts.

A life philosophy of denial and repression ultimately misses reality. Whoever closes his eyes to suffering ceases to live. Love, limitations, illness, and death are the fundamental experiences of human existence. Love and death: they are life, and life hurts. Suffering in itself is meaningless but it serves as a ground for protesting and for fighting deprivation and misery. We must avoid deprivation and misery with all our might and seek to abolish them!

The Courage to Fail

We are meant to do every day what is possible in our small sphere of influence. Involvement and the readiness to withstand frustrations are probably core virtues needed for survival.

Every day I see uncountable opportunities to do these little things—gestures that make me happy and make those happy for whom I do them. Does not our Lord call us "blessed"? In the New Testament, the second part of the Holy Book of Christians, it reads, "I was hungry and you gave me to eat. I was thirsty and you gave me to drink. I was without shelter and you took me in. I was naked and you gave me clothing." Concrete social action, nothing pious or showy, nothing even difficult. Small everyday gestures aimed at concrete reduction of material need.

But then the quotation continues and now it suddenly sounds different: "I was sick and you visited me. I was in jail and you came to me." It does not say, "You diagnosed my sickness and found a new drug or a

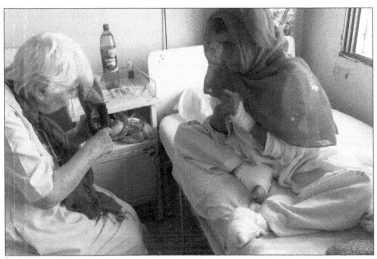
Dr. Pfau visits with a patient.

vaccine so that others would not be infected." It does not say, "You must heal the sick of their illnesses." And it also does not say that I must liberate prisoners, though we have to do all these things too, with full attention.

But there are patients whom we no longer can cure. There are people in jail who have been sentenced according to the law. There is nothing we can do to change the situation. We are nevertheless called to not turn our faces.

Perhaps that has been one of my most important existential experiences: even in helplessness there is a hidden possibility and significance. In our work in Afghanistan we, of course, could not force the Russians into retreat. Nor can we leprosy workers transform the unjust structures of the world, or even of Pakistan. What is decisive is that we are here nevertheless and share their suffering with them.

> Even in helplessness there is a hidden
> possibility and significance.

Our work in the war-torn section of Afghanistan began at point zero. There was nothing we could do except caress the young wounded soldiers on the forehead in the gentle way that their mothers would have done it. And hold their hands. We could not save their lives because there were simply no blood transfusions available. Yet our effort had meaning because human contact with one another is meaningful even when effective medical help is not possible.

You visited me. Naturally we did not just stand there in Pakistan and Afghanistan with the impulse to show compassion. Naturally, we thought through the situation strategically. Naturally, we entered our epidemiological data in Pakistan into a computer.

Once we get beyond the first steps, we still carry, of course, our culture and our training with us. We do that automatically. But often already in this first step love begins to seem futile. It can only be preserved and only prove itself in its essence when it is maintained in the face of futility. That is something that does not fit into the categories of our achievement society. Yet it is central for MALC to do something that actually does not bring obvious results. Those who only see the structures that cannot be changed, those who slide into apathy when there is not a solution for everything, those who have no understanding that you have to begin again and again and again—those persons have not loved.

If Christians do not have the courage to be crazy, to be fools for Christ—if they always ask, "What is this useful for?" rather than "What is this good for?"—what is Christianity good for?

> If Christians do not have the courage to be crazy, to be fools for Christ—if they always ask, "What is this useful for?" rather than "What is this good for?"—what is Christianity good for?

On the day of final judgment, we shall be asked whether we were crazy like He was, whether we gave ourselves unreservedly to him who was destroyed and was "a loser"—and who through all that redeemed us. If we do not have the courage to fail, if we do not have the courage to stand by when a cancer patient dies or by a homeless person or a drug addict of whom we know we cannot resocialize, if we do not have the courage to say to our spouse, even when it is difficult, or to a child when we have not planned its coming, to say yes and "good that you came into my life," then how are we ever going to have the courage to let the craziness of love come into our society?

11

About Suffering, Norms, Limits, and Freedom

1984: The Experience during the Desert Pilgrimage

Hassan grins surprised and sighs with relief when we once again pull off a miraculous escape: a shepherd's tent that went up during the night. We narrowly escaped machine gun fire. We suddenly made out in front of us the tracks left by a truck, just as we believed we had lost our way in the wilderness. We will never forget, Hassan and I, how we traveled "under the wings of the Most High," how "a cloud hovered over us during the day, and a pillar of fire during the night."

When I traveled into Afghanistan in 1987, I felt strangely lonely. That time there was no accompanying protection of the mujahideens; there was no vehicle for us. That vehicle had been our tiny possession, an illusion of a private sphere in which we could sleep and live and even hold consultations when it was necessary. This time we traveled by public transport: a rickety pickup, where they gave me the "seat of honor" on the engine box.

It was spring then and the snow had just melted. Spring flowers were blooming—white, yellow, pink, blue.

In the early nineties, I was in Afghanistan once again. With each visit, I had a stronger impression of the experience of suffering.

An entire people were oppressed, and they suffered without the world rising to help them. This is a people for whom independence and freedom are the highest values. Afghanistan is a country that had never been conquered or colonized. Whenever aggressors in the past managed to penetrate it, they were never able to rule it. An entire people was somehow drawn into a conflict between the great powers, without those affected ever being asked about it, without them being able to defend themselves. Who had ever asked these mountain farmers, these women and children, all these little people who had never wanted this conflict? Was the public opinion ever concerned about them?

The Russians were supposedly called into the country (1979–80) in order to help the Afghan Socialist government with "the liberation of the people from reactionary forces." From the beginning, the Afghani resistance movement was convinced that it was conducting a holy war against unbelievers, thus compromises were not possible.

My concern was not the politic of the resistance. My concern pertained to the people—a people participating in the resistance against their own government and with no hospitals, no schools, no public transportation, no banks, no post office, no legal system. Here people had to die because the infrastructure had collapsed. The people of this poor country had been cut off from their own resources. Today, normally, children who have diarrhea do not have to die. Today, someone suffering blood loss does not have to die. We Westerners establish policies so that in our later years we can be provided for. Why then should these people not be provided for, medically, when they are facing acute and life-threatening injuries?

When we have contempt for war as the means of continuing politics then that attitude should not apply only to us. Especially here, where it is not a matter of two enemy armies battling against each other. Especially here, where no war has been declared. Here a government was supported by a world power against the civilian population.

What did not let me sleep was that people I encountered in Afghanistan had no voices—*they had no voices.*

"Our words are gone with the wind." In 1987, when I traveled from Afghanistan directly to Germany, my youngest colleague, John, said to me, "You must shout about what you've seen here. When we do not cry out day after day, we who are confronted with this insanity, who then will do it? Write something. You must write. You must tell the world what the people here endure, how they're dying."

Afghanistan: The Violet Thistles

When I came to Afghanistan again in 1989 it was high summer. Most of the mountain streams were dry and the sun had mercilessly dried up the land and dried out the spring flowers. Only the thorns had survived and the mountain brushes, too. Their rough surface protected them. The goat herds did not risk touching them. It annoyed me that these thorns were the only ones that had succeeded with their philosophy of aggression.

Then the unexpected happened. First in one bush, then two, then in entire fields: the thorns produced buds. And then the buds opened and an over-filled bunch of soft violet flowers with tender blooming leaves came out—defenseless, soft, fragrant. The cradled blooming heads attracted butterflies—butterflies over slopes covered by thorny thistles.

I thought pensively, how beautiful that these thorns have survived, that they have a chance to reveal their secret: these vulnerable, soft, blooming violet flowers that nobody ever thought these thistles would be able to bring forth and without which, defenseless and soft, there would be no future for them at all.

Afghanistan is a dangerous but also violent country. I experienced violence not only in Pakistan but also in the Afghani civil war. Nevertheless, what occurs in Afghanistan is rather different from what occurs in Gilgit and from what we have experienced in Karachi. In the maze of Afghanistan and in the provincial areas, though no longer in Kabul, there are still tribal laws. These laws are harsh but they bind human beings to norms. In Kabul, however, women are raped and naked terror rules the day. Everything is destroyed in the big cities. But in central Afghanistan where we work, people know what can happen if norms are violated. The situation is indeed still crazy and brutal, but one can, as a rule, prepare the team for situations they will encounter.

The Afghans at least can interpret it and understand it all, though we may not comprehend it at all.

Afghanistan is too alien for me to have invested my life there. That applies less so in my relationships to leprosy technicians and leprosy patients. We have gone together through too many hardships, adventures, beautiful and sad moments, to still feel strange to one another.

That is not all. Afghanis are hungry for the values we live. There is Zahir's life history:

When I was six, I had a friend. A fair boy, beaming with zest for life, always ready to start a new adventure. One night, when I was eight, I overheard the discussion of the village elders. Salim, they said, had contracted leprosy. Leprosy was such a dangerous disease, a curse of God. The patient should not be allowed to live. Salim was to be drowned in the river.

I have not seen my friend again.

Had he heard the verdict? Had his mother succeeded in saving his life? I didn't dare ask. But I made up my mind: when I grew up, I would see that these patients would get their right to live! And then, when I did grow up, you came to Afghanistan.

Or Qurban's story. Once, we reviewed the five to ten years we had worked in Hazarajat. "What has made us invincible," Qurban said, "so that nobody could do anything against us, is our defenselessness. We don't sport Kalashinkovs, we don't fight back, we don't argue. We help people, anyone who needs our help. And therefore we are still here." Here, in central Afghanistan, we are the only NGO (nongovernmental organization) that has been able to continue reasonably undisturbed for ten years.

But the group dynamics, the ways in which they interact with one another, are completely incomprehensible to me. For instance, there is the story of Ibrahim, the uncle of leprosy technician Jawad. Ibrahim completed his school-leaving certificate but he had no formal medical training. Jawad brought him to us at the very beginning of our project.

Ibrahim had always worked as a bazaar doctor and has considerable experience in what one should do in certain medical cases. He does not know, for example, why something should be sewed together, but in the case of an injury his stitches are excellent. He also joins the right tissue structures. He was the first of the entire team whom I taught how one operates on eyelids that are paralyzed by leprosy and unable to close, and he did it very well.

We hired him but we explained from the beginning that he could not work with Jawad in the same outpatient station: "The uncle cannot work under his nephew. That is against all of your tribal customs." Jawad, however, spoke out decisively about his tribe and, because he understands the situation in Afghanistan better than we do, we believed him. Still, we insisted on our contractual conditions.

When Jawad then began to work at his home station, his uncle Ibrahim suddenly showed up there. We explained clearly that he did not have a vacant post there. He answered, "How is this possible? This is my home village."

At the end we had to release him because he was violating our orders. A transfer was simply not possible. Subsequently, Ibrahim organized his tribe and chased LEPCO (the name of our leprosy organization) away from the outpatient station and took control of our convoy with his own people. Later he came to our headquarters and said he felt awfully sorry about the entire story. "But what else could I have done?" he asked. Today he is hired once again.

Or what about Sadiq? He worked alone in his outpatient station. Suddenly he declared that he had to visit his family in Iran, where they had fled. Iran was expelling all Afghanis so we, therefore, were able to sympathize with his aim. But it was not possible to explain to him that there were consequences for our work linked to his decision. What would happen in the meantime? Who could replace him? Why did he not wait until the successor staff came back in three months from their training? He could not understand that. Because he did not get his vacation request, he submitted his resignation, adding, "In April I'll be back." It was self-evident to him that we would take him back.

Birthday Party during the Teaching Camp

I have no idea how they found out the date of my birthday. It was in September during the teaching camp in Lal. During the nights it was already bitterly cold with frost. In August the window bolts froze shut and it was not possible to heat the rooms. Once again, we had an unforeseen number of patients and there were only tents to house them. While we were doing the rounds, the wind howled through the tents.

My sixty-fifth birthday fell into this time. The morning began with the team bringing me three golden dandelion flowers. They had already found that many but they would look further so that they would be able to have an entire bouquet. In the course of the day, they gathered up all available flowers they could find within a radius of three kilometers (almost two miles). Then they built a birthday table, decorated an honorary chair, and had a Spanish cover put up; they had got it out of the clinic.

They had also got a wine-red pullover as a present for me. Wine-red is my favorite color. The pullover clearly came from Germany. It must have been acquired by a donation intended for the incoming refugees, bought up in Pakistan, and then sold, so that it had finally landed in a bazaar in Lal. It cost about seventy-five cents there. It is a beautiful, warm woolly that I still wear today. I was really overjoyed about it.

Then came the best thing—an envelope colored with flowers and with the following words written on it: "Each one of us presents you with three years of our life. Ten times three makes thirty, and with that you can do for Afghanistan exactly the same that you have done for Pakistan."

And then, despite my protests, they slaughtered a baby goat and a young lamb and we ate well and celebrated with gusto.

The only thing I could not move them to do was dance. They never dance when women are around.

Only when we women withdrew did the "proper" atmosphere arise for the men, with its customary wild abandon.

On this evening I was very happy.

1 2

Working for Peace in Karachi

Rocket Launchers and Russian Rifles

The area around Gilgit had, for a long time, been the most peaceful province of all Pakistan, and that was still true as late as the 1980s. Karachi has gone through a similar development. In the past, people in this city married across the boundaries of their tribes: a Pathan would marry a Balochi woman, a Balochi man would marry a Punjabi, and all Pakistan looked at Karachi in fascination and said, "What is possible in Karachi will one day also be possible in the rest of Pakistan."

An escalation of violence has in the meantime turned this once blooming trading center into a city of terror and death.

I made these notations in my journal.

New Year's Eve in 1996, a new beginning, nothing written on that page yet, it is white and promising ...

January 2nd, 1996. Seventeen casualties from terrorist acts. The house of a milkman was robbed in broad daylight. As if a milkman earned a lot! What is there to steal in his house! If they did not put up any resistance, and did not talk to the police, the robbers had said, nothing would happen to the family. How can you put up resistance if the intruders are armed with machine guns? And then, before they left, the robbers put seven male members of the family against the wall and shot them, in cold blood—the father, his brother, five children. Now is the month of Ramadan, the month of fasting, we sigh a sigh of relief—a break in the terror, that is at least what we hope.

I must not think about the mother of those murdered children. How much empathy can you afford without losing your mind?

January 3rd. Today, Bashir's house was robbed. They took valuables, money, and his motorbike. And finally they issued a warning in case the police were informed. Bashir is a longtime employee of our clinic, a leprosy assistant who is responsible for the physical therapy in the hospital. He has four children and now deems himself lucky that nothing happened to any member of his family.

The new year goes on as the last one ended. Karachi has become a jungle of violence and murder. An atmosphere of hate and fear rules the city, which is governed by Kalashnikovs (Russian rifles) and rocket launchers. Each day, there are more casualties due to terrorist activities in this city than there are in the war ravaging Bosnia. The murders by the gangs are spreading fear everywhere. One murdered child is enough to make a city with millions of inhabitants panic and to paralyze all life.

No family in the whole city dares to send their children to school after such a day.

Fear and Terror

The long-smouldering conflict in Karachi has developed into an open state of war between the extremists and the government. A permanent state of fear prevails, which tortures the common people most of all.

The reasons for the conflict are complex and tangled. Many seem comprehensible, others utterly irrational.

At the beginning of February 1996, I flew to Germany. The last gruesome Karachi murder happened just before my departure. We found the torso of a child, two days later the legs, another two days later the arms. When I left, the head had not yet been found.

What have we done so that these young men do not have any inhibitions anymore? As a doctor, I know that you cannot do such a thing inconspicuously and easily. The murderers must have been spattered with blood from head to toe when they cut the body apart. If people with such low inhibition levels are walking about in Karachi, anything can happen.

Terror at All Levels

Spring 1996. The climate of violence has also reached our project. Dr. Tobias, who is responsible for the medical side of the leprosy project, is suddenly faced with a difficult dilemma. He received horrifying threats against his life, the most disgusting threats I have ever read: "We will tie you up, the members of our group will all rape your wife before your eyes, we will kill your son, and then we will administer you the *coup de grace*." I have been assured that someone only wanted to take revenge verbally.

In a situation characterized by terror, however, many people see a chance to settle personal scores. The outcome of these threats was impossible to predict, and therefore serious—deadly serious. Dr. Tobias had ignored two letters but the daily urban terror remained as a frightening background. After the third letter, he said, "I can't stand this anymore." We sent him and his family out of country. Now we have to ask ourselves, how can we go on in such a situation? What can we do?

The History of the Bihari

You have to reconstruct the very complex and obscure historical background to understand what is behind the slogan of revenge and violence. You have to know where there was injustice in the past to grasp the explosive situation in this city today. There are many different strands, which are entwined.

First there is the situation of the Bihari. These Indian immigrants, who came to Pakistan in 1947, are called "refugees" to this day. They are Muslims who emigrated from mainly Hindu India to the newly founded Islamic Pakistan, streaming into Karachi. In 1971, during the pogroms, those cruelties and horrid mass killings that preceded the founding of Bangladesh, the second wave of Bihari refugees came into Pakistan. They mainly settled in Orangi, an outlying district of Karachi, in the desert belt next to Balochistan, a part of town that has become, with over a million inhabitants, probably the largest slum in the world.

Through our work we soon had close contact to this group of refugees. Among them there are ten times more leprosy patients than in the native population. At that time, I went to Orangi quite often, and I was fascinated again and again. While they were still living in tents, they had already organized neighborhood trade and barter economies. They built emergency accommodations consisting of two rooms, one of which they used as a workshop while living in the other. They made toy cars for two rupees; they made plastic items, everything that was useful and could be sold at the local market. This group built their own sewage system in the slum. The Bihari were not given the official status of refugees and thus did not receive any international aid. This status is reserved for those fleeing from one country into another. The Bihari, however, came as refugees from the same country. Bangladesh was then still part of Pakistan, therefore there was no aid from the United Nations. And since there was no help from outside, these people had to save themselves.

I still remember the first mass screening for leprosy there. We went from tent to tent. The women sat there—most of the men had died or were prisoners of war—with their children around the cold fireplace. When we told them, "We can do more for you than just provide this leprosy program," the reaction was spontaneous, clear, and typical: "We want a school for our children." These Bihari, a group that was soon

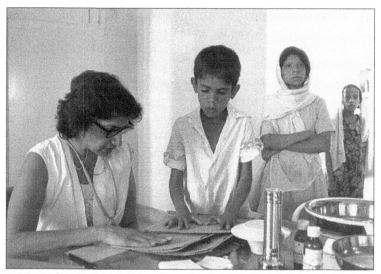

Originally from Bombay, dermatologist Dr. Zarina Fazelbhoy, a longtime MALC colleague, at work in a MALC outpost in Bihar Colony, an extremely overpopulated, socially vulnerable part of Karachi. Photo: DAHW, Hans Kutnewsky

rising economically as well as socially, were later excluded from participating in the political affairs of Pakistan. When they started to organize
their own political party, we were full of hope. It was the only party,
and still is, that was not dominated by feudal landowners; it was a real
citizens' party. However, in spite of their education level being higher
than average (we have recruited many of our leprosy assistants from
this group of Bihari), the discrimination against them remained. Dr.
Zarina, a dermatologist and longtime volunteer of the program, once
told me: "My son, who was born in Karachi, is still being called *muhajir*,
which means 'refugee.' After thirty-six years." Thus, in the early seventies, they reinterpreted the discriminating term positively in politics,
joining together in the political party called Muhajir Qaumi Movement
(MQM). *Qaumi* actually means "tribe," thus also includes the demand
for home rule. When this group organized the basis of this claim, it was
obvious that there was a new power in society that would have to be
taken seriously.

By then Karachi had already been a city politically topsy-turvy for
some decades. Amid the violent demonstrations, all of a sudden you
could see these MQM boys distributing flowers. Flowers instead of bullets. They formed groups, which, for example, swept their streets on
their own initiative, cleared the sewage pipes, paved streets, built play-
grounds for the children, planted trees. It really was a wonderful movement—in the beginning. I dreamed: Pakistan is growing up politically.
It still breaks my heart when I think about the constructive opportunities that have been wasted. Of course, there was envy. But was there
anything the representatives of the central government, many of them
rich feudal landowners, had to fear from these enterprises?

I remember Tohid Colony clearly, where we went from house to
house in 1971. We drew a street map for our mass screening because
there was none. When I came back to Orangi in 1997, the houses were
barricaded in reaction to the brutal aggression of the gang of thugs
patrolling the neighborhood. Frightened inhabitants existed behind
boarded-up windows and locked doors.

My heart was bleeding.

I did not follow closely what happened after the party was founded,
since I was mostly working in the provinces at that time. However, violence was escalating over the years on all sides. The political organization

of the Bihari was connected with the painful experiences of a minority that had been persecuted again and again. They were victims when the Sindhi (a people living in the Sindh region), turned against these rising miniature entrepreneurs. They were herded into the market hall, which was set on fire on four corners. No newspaper ever publicized how many perished that day. After this pogrom-like assault, the *muhajir* went underground. We later tracked many of our Bihari leprosy patients down, providing them treatment in the rural areas of Sindh, one after the other.

For years, nothing special happened. Then the clashes flared up once again. In the late seventies and early eighties, a violent conflict arose between the Pathans and the Indian immigrants, again because of economic reasons. The core of the conflict: the Pathans were then about to monopolize trade in Karachi. The Bihari now disputed this monopoly. The Pathans lived up in the hills around Karachi; the Bihari lived in the lower areas. The Pathans, members of heavily armed mountain tribes who traditionally prove their masculinity with their guns, were attacking from the hills. The military sealed off the whole area to secure order. The shooting lasted for days. At that time I already was a government health advisor, therefore we could enter the hard-fought area with our ambulance to distribute food to our employees and the patients who lived there. None of them could leave the battle zone to buy food supplies.

On this occasion, a group of young men stopped us. "What are you doing here?"

Pir Ali, who was driving our car, kept his cool. "We are carrying food supplies for our patients. Do you object?"

The answer was unexpectedly aggressive. "Damn it, you should not bring food! Bring us weapons!"

I was horrified. That was something I had never heard from that group—never! All these people had wanted before were schools, to trade, and to live in peace.

Some days later, the situation grew really explosive. The Pathans sent their families back to their villages, and the Bihari packed their bags and went on their way.

We asked them uncomprehendingly, "Where are you going?"

"There must be a place in Pakistan, they said, where our children can live in safety. We will search for one."

> That has haunted me ever since, that there
> was a group of people who had fled from India
> to Bangladesh, and then from Bangladesh to
> Pakistan. And now they had to become refugees
> again.... They had no place to go, no "home."

That has haunted me ever since, that there was a group of people who had fled from India to Bangladesh, and then from Bangladesh to Pakistan. And now they had to become refugees again, after they had just built themselves an existence through their hard work. They had no place to go, no "home."

After that everything seemed to go back to normal. Under General Muhammad Zia-ul-Haq there was little opportunity for political expression. But the peace was illusory. When the conflicts flared up again, the Bihari had learned from the past and had supplied themselves with arms.

Their political party, which had originally aimed at developing Karachi, was slowly sliding into the opposite role. Now they only wanted to destroy. Their fundamental experience was this: if we are not the first ones to attack, we will be shot down. Their second experience: even if we successfully organize ourselves politically, we are not accepted as a group and we are also not strong enough to defend ourselves against repression. A high portion of qualified yet unemployed young people increased the pressure. In a country where 75 percent of the population is illiterate, you are counted among the intellectual elite if you graduated from college.

Sociologists explain the escalation of violence in Karachi this way: it is all about the clash between rural feudal structures and the evolving urban middle class. In 1947, 80 percent of the Pakistani population still lived in the countryside. Now it is 60 percent. By 2020, it is estimated that only 30 percent will live there. The feudal landowners cling to their power. In Karachi, this anachronism first turned into violence when the new immigrant groups were refused their share of power. At the municipal elections in the late eighties, MQM had actually won considerably in Karachi. Then it all started: as soon as the MQM had the majority in the city parliament, they put their people in all the important positions.

The Sindhi, to whom the province of Sindh "originally belonged," felt completely marginalized. An extraparliamentary opposition taking over government responsibilities has to prove that it is able to follow political rules. The MQM obviously failed there. However, they should have been given time to learn. So the evolving middle class was driven underground and there they learned the trade of terrorism.

The central government, characterized by feudalism, was engaging in stronger and stronger reprisals in the early nineties. The executive authorities in Islamabad sent the army to Karachi in 1992 to prevent further escalation of the conflicts. When the army left, the Ranger paramilitary forces stayed behind. That was the beginning of a cruel war in the city. In 1995, according to official statements, 2,052 people died due to politically motivated shootings and acts of violence, among them many innocent bystanders.

In 1995, three factors determined the civil war–like situation: the violent fight of the political parties, the counterviolence and the state terror of the Rangers, and also criminal elements, who in this chaotic situation always try to get a piece of the cake for themselves.

Party Strife and Civil War

First of all, the political parties: the central government succeeded in dividing the formerly united people's movement of the MQM into two parties. After the MQM had been turned out of parliament, the movement split. Next to the MQM, a second party, the Haqiqi, was established—the name means "the actual ones." Of the MQM, which had originally been ethnically formed, today only a small rump party is left. The Haqiqi had at first been courted by the government but was then turned out of parliament as well. The MQM and the Haqiqi now fight each other to the last, therefore they are no longer dangerous for the central government. But for Karachi, the potential for danger has doubled. There are now two groups of terrorists who want to prove to the population which is the more dangerous of the two.

Do the MQM and the Haqiqi have any political objectives? Maybe they are trying to make Karachi the sixth province of Pakistan, a political region where they have home rule. When their leader, Altaf Hussain, indeed a führer, makes a call from his London exile, the whole city is on strike the next day. His word is law for the MQM, which strictly adheres to the principles of hierarchy. He stirs up emotions with seductive slogans taken from Hitler: "You are a people without space." A high-ranking MQM politician admitted, "If he said, 'Go and drown yourselves in the sea,' 70 percent of the Muhajir would follow him." That is very characteristic of the emotional and political situation.

Whatever the official programs of both parties proclaim today, one of the true main objectives is to make money. Terrorists from each party have actually conquered different parts of Karachi, district after district, street after street, collecting taxes in each of their territories. In Landhi, the Haqiqi rule the whole area. Wherever they are in control, they confiscate a villa, paint it white, hoist their flag, open their headquarters, and call it the "White House." In G11, a part of New Karachi, the Haqiqi control certain streets while the adjacent rows of houses are ruled by the MQM. At the entrance of each street, the young freedom fighters have barricaded themselves behind sandbags. Like warlords, they have distributed everything among them. Then everything is pilfered ruthlessly, everything that is not nailed down. Unfortunately, the police assist them. The population cannot defend itself; there is nothing the people can do.

13

The Struggle Against
Terror and Violence

Counterterror

To fight these terrorist groups, a most brutal form of state terror has emerged. That is the second strand of the violent situation. The Rangers, a paramilitary intervention squad of the police, were deployed after the army had not been able to control the riots and had been withdrawn. The members of this force are active players in this tragedy of impotence, terror, and death. They comb through whole districts, terrorizing the people. They completely seal off parts of the city and search them for weapons. A whole age group is simply arrested and imprisoned. People are beaten until they make a statement. Executions occur without trials or sentences.

Matthias, one of our young employees, had been in one of these prisons. He had suddenly disappeared, picked up in one of these police raids only because he was of a "conspicuous" age. For two days we searched for him desperately in all of Karachi. On the third day, he arrived at the hospital at 4 a.m., still in his pajamas. They had taken him away without telling his family. After he was arrested, he was interrogated for two days.

When the Rangers are conducting one of their raids, they take all the young men between the ages of eighteen and thirty-five. They arrive at 3 a.m., sift through a whole district, breaking into and entering every house. Anyone could end up in their clutches. The police kept Denver, the administration director of our MALC clinic, for five days before we could get him out again.

What was the reason for his arrest? His nephew, a Catholic youngster, had run off with a Muslim girl and, according to the principles of the clan whereby all the members of a family are liable for the crimes of one member, the uncle and his daughter were arrested, both without a warrant.

The girl was sent home after a day. He had not been maltreated himself, he said. He told us that shortly before his arrest, five rockets had been fired at the government buildings in Karachi in the middle of the day. To this day, nobody knows where these heavy arms came from; after all, they cannot simply be thrown out a car window. The Rangers had interrogated by torture a great number of suspects in the same prison in which Denver was locked up. He had to listen to their screams for five days and nights, twenty-four hours a day. He told me, "I almost lost my mind."

The young men recruited for the Rangers are used for murder and other acts of violence. However, they live under extreme pressure themselves, in permanent mortal danger. With unemployment being so high, many take on any form of work, even that. Sometimes the terrorists' violence is only directed at the Rangers. At such time, nobody is shot except Rangers, nobody is kidnapped except them. At other times, it is the civilian population's turn again, and after that the political opponents' turn. You never know what is on the agenda at what time.

Additional Conflicts

And then the third strand: in this brutal atmosphere, in the anonymity of the city, additional conflicts flare up, old enmities are dealt with through violence. The victims are, as ever, the poor, the women, and the children.

There is blackmailing, old scores are settled; there are acts of revenge that can be blamed on the terrorists. The religious aspect is of no importance in this street war. The immigrants are not Hindus, after all. They fled from India because of their Muslim religion. They argue, "We are the only Pakistanis. The others are either Sindhi, Balochis, or Pathans. Yet we are Pakistanis. This is our identity."

However, religious differences are exploited and used politically. It happens once in a while that they shoot directly at a mosque. Recently, there were twenty-one casualties when they fired into a prayer group in a mosque. Such an incident is then presented as a war between Shia and Sunnis.

When acts of violence are directed at the civil population, pure terror rules. When a child, utterly mutilated, is sent to his parents in pieces sown in bags, after a long time of waiting, after threatening letters and announcements, then a single murder like that is enough to take the population of a whole city as hostage.

Each faction possesses an armed force of only five thousand men; there are no more than that. With these numbers, only acts of terror can be committed but they know well how to do that.

Then there are those who take part in attacks only from time to time, though admittedly not in such perverted atrocities. They will tell you plainly: "My family was in debt. I had to earn money somehow, and I can't do it any other way. And now I am already able to pay back the debts of my family after two weeks."

The Role of the Victim Is Reversed

When the terror had not yet reached the center of Karachi and was still in the rural areas of Sindh, you could read advertisements such as this one in the newspapers: "We are looking for young people who are able to use modern means of communication, very good pay, Box number XYZ."

Everyone knew what that meant. Organized gangs sat in the impenetrable jungle along the Indus, testing the methods that they later introduced into the city's guerrilla war. The era is passed when highwaymen killed people only in self-defense, and if they killed people, they did it quickly. The organized political gangs want to destabilize the political order and the ruling government, and they certainly want to prove one thing: "We are the ones who really are in power in Karachi." Their fight is successful, though it is fought on the backs of the common people. Twice a week a general strike is announced: nobody can go to work or send their children to school; the water and the electricity supplies are cut off. Since a huge portion of Karachi lives on some small trade, the people are without income on such days. Unemployment rises even higher, the industries move to the Punjab.

I have lived in Muhajir areas for some weeks, when I stayed successively in two of our outstations. It is always the same. In the afternoon, it is still quiet around the leprosy control unit. Then, in the evening, jeeps drive through the area, booming from their loudspeakers: "Tomorrow is a strike. If anyone is seen on the street and shot, it is his own fault." In Karachi, half a dozen or a dozen vehicles, whether buses or private cars, are torched during the evening preceding the strike, just to be on the safe side. Gestures of violence show "You'd better really take this seriously tomorrow."

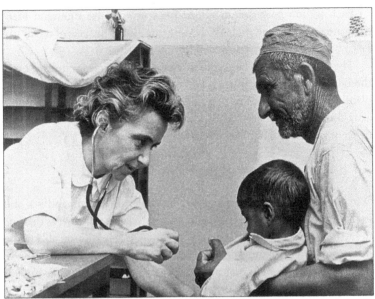

In addition to the obligations at MALC, Dr. Pfau provided free medical care for the poor in Baldia, a large suburb of Karachi. Photo: DAHW, Hans Kutnewsky

Even among the many sympathizers of the Muhajir, more and more find it unbearable that the economy of Karachi is being totally destroyed by these strikes. The people are getting tired of it.

It is certainly important to analyze and understand the background of the situation. However, I shall never be able to understand the coldness of this killing, and I am terribly upset by it. For example, young men are looking for shelter in a house. They say the police are after them. The family takes them in, lets them stay the night, and even serves them breakfast. They eat calmly. After breakfast, they make the male members of the family, adults and children, stand against the wall. They shoot them all, simply shoot them down, utterly cool and deliberate. In the past, there was shooting of identified enemies. Children and civilians got into the crossfire, their deaths were accepted. Today, they kill very purposefully but utterly unpredictably. They do not storm into the offices of their political enemies and shoot their rifles until empty. This no longer is the aggressive reflex toward the adversary. Someone is kidnapped, tortured, and finally killed. There is no definite concept of "the enemy."

We know that man has an instinct for hunting. I can even understand this somehow. But that people can sit down in the evening, planning a murder right down to the last detail in cold blood, as if they were thinking, "What's up tomorrow?"—that is perverse. The more innocent the victim, the more fear is generated by such a murder. The terrorists' aim is to get society into their clutches. The victim's role is reversed; people who regard themselves as victims become perpetrators. "Take revenge!"—this slogan of blind hatred characterizes the violence of Karachi. The victim is really only a means to the end of blind, cold-blooded, and deliberate destruction.

Not to Become Indifferent

However, we should not grow arrogant. Auschwitz, the place of coolly planned destruction, had been devised by educated people. What upsets me in Karachi is not a new experience for me, as a German. Yet this repeated, close experience permits no suppression, the kind of suppression you can possibly practice for a lifetime in Germany.

Auschwitz, Golgotha, Karachi—it should not have been, and still it has been. It still is.

In a letter I wrote at that time to a friend:

I didn't dare to look for years, for decades. I don't know if you can understand this. Of course you can't understand it if I can't put it into words. You can't put madness into words. Can you stammer it? If life is like *that*—if it can be like *that* at any time—do you understand that I am not able to look into that abyss? And I still must look because it is the truth that life is like that. And because only the truth can set us free. Free.

If life is like *that*—if it can be like *that* at any
time—do you understand that I am not able
to look into that abyss? And I still must look
because it is the truth that life is like that. And
because only the truth can set us free. Free.

I have to look because it is the only way to escape indifference. Indifference, says the writer Elie Wiesel (and, as an Auschwitz survivor, he must know better than any of us), is the true sin. Hate still has something of humanity in it; victim and perpetrator are still connected by feelings, dark feelings that should not exist but do exist. But even for the perpetrator, the existence of the victim is not denied. To the indifferent person, the victim does not even exist in the negative sense.

I must not look away. I have to have the courage to look, to be hurt in my memory.

Morning in Karachi. E. is glancing through the newspaper.

"Four casualties yesterday," he notes tersely. The news story is on the back page; on the front page there are only the two-digit numbers.

"Not more?" says M. "Yesterday there were eleven."

"One is too much, much too much," I burst out. "Much too much."

Before my eyes I see the mother who receives the news.

How much empathy can you afford and still accept the early song of the blackbird as a present and the overwhelming red of the hibiscus flowers?

Against indifference—especially today, when the news overwhelms us—I have to look and bear it; I have to accept reality: man is not necessarily good. I have to stand by the tears that I have not cried because I can only reach part of the truth through them. It is not the whole truth to which they connect me, but it is truth and, as such, life. Maybe this fact has changed for me in my older age. I am now better able to look, to give this life a chance, and thus to snatch it from indifference.

Why did Golgotha have to be? I have seen too much, too much. I am not able to indulge in illusions as to what happened there. I cannot sleep under a crucifix; when I am in Germany, I always have to put it in the closet, reverently. I cannot endure this domesticated image. Golgotha should not have been, and still it has been. Why? I do not know. All I know is that it has been and that I, if I looked away, would thereby abandon to indifference something very precious. I do not even know what this important something is but it still must not be forgotten.

And then I go to the ward again at 10 p.m., to Paul, even though I know that he does not recognize me anymore and that he will mumble something with his dry lips that will be incomprehensible to me. I drip a spoonful of water into his parched mouth. He cannot swallow anymore, the intravenous feeding continues without really giving him relief. For three weeks Paul has been dying, and we can help him so little. It is easy to forget him—there are seventy-nine more patients in the ward for whom we can still do something.

I write in the letter to my friend in Germany: "Do you understand that this has something to do with my outcry against indifference? The way we treat the dying?"

14

Karachi—City of Death

Miracles in the Metropolitan Jungle

I have changed plans for the near future. The trips to the mountain massif of the north or the desert areas in the south of Pakistan or even into Afghanistan ravaged by war are no longer on my list of priorities. My time and my devotion will belong to Karachi.

I have avoided this city for a long time. It was in Karachi that I first transferred responsibility fully into local hands. Only now have I really gone to Karachi, and only because I had to. I did not like the city.

Then came the year when Dr. Tobias received the murder threats, so he was happy when I returned. I thought, if I have to be in Karachi anyway, I might as well try to make the best of the time here. Once I got started, I could not stop.

Thus my place was no longer in the quiet forests of Azad Kashmir or in the deserted mountain farms of the Hindu Kush, where the moon at night makes the glaciers shine in a silvery light. My place was in Karachi, the city of thirteen million inhabitants, which had been brought to the edge by violence and a war between brothers.

After one of my last long survey tours in the Kashmir region, my sister in religion, Jeannine, picked me up at the airport. We exchanged news with that dry humor that has often helped us cope in difficult situations. My first day in the hospital, I did not even have time to open my computer. Employees, patients, members of the training course came in one after the other. Some things are simply wonderful—Ilyas only came to say thank you. He was involved in embezzlement and was laid off. That lapse changed his life. He paid back the money and we finally persuaded the administration to give him another chance. "Pray for me," he said when he left.

Zubeida did not even say thank you as our paths crossed on the stairs, but the smile that she gave me expressed everything. Her husband, involved in the same matter, was also granted probation. To be sacked in the present situation of the labor market, with only a qualification as a leprosy technician and without any unemployment insurance, means abject misery.

And then there were the actual problems. I only listened. I could not offer solutions anyway. Yet when the patients finally got up, they said thank you with relief in their voices. Who in today's Karachi takes the time to listen, merely to listen?

Through the Ghost City at Night

In the evening, at 8 p.m., I decide to drive to our noviciate after all. I had promised them at Mass that morning at 6 a.m. that I would spend the night there. Our guards look at me in disbelief, "Doctor, there is no one on the streets." My heart flutters. Yet I know that if I do not act normally from the beginning I will spend half of my time during the next months calculating the security risk, and that does not really work anyway. If I simply live as always in these five months to come, I will gain as much experience concerning the Karachi jungle laws as I did in Afghanistan. Therefore, I drive to the noviciate. It is a complete success. Normally, it takes thirty-five minutes to get through the traffic jams at 8 p.m. Today I bet I can do it in twelve minutes.

I make it in eleven. Half an hour later, the machine guns start to chatter but by that time we are already sitting in the chapel at the weekly prayer for peace. Unmoved by the outside events, the young novices sing the litany of supplication with special fervor.

The shooting goes on sporadically through the whole night. Not yet used to the laws of the jungle of Karachi, I do not know whether to sleep all dressed, as I did in Afghanistan in similar situations, or to ignore it. Finally I decide on a compromise: the dressing gown. In a dressing gown I can run out quickly if necessary.

Around 3 a.m. the shooting dies down. At 5 a.m. there is morning prayer in the chapel. At 6 a.m. we want to drive to Manghopir. At 5:45 a.m. the shooting starts again. It takes us until 7 a.m. before we can get the necessary report about the situation: in the city center, the violence continues. Farther on, in the outskirts, in the direction of Manghopir, the situation has calmed down again. So I drive, this time without the novices. But they can pack the cooking pots into the car and then I will at least have this pleasant surprise for the school in Manghopir.

It is like Afghanistan. In the dim light of early morning, everybody coming toward my car is a potential attacker. The streets are empty; I can drive fifty miles per hour in the middle of the city. Only in Golimar do I change into second, then first gear, because of the slalom course forced on me. They have even pulled out the metal bars dividing the lane; they lie bent everywhere on the ground, amid stones, bricks, burnt tires, and splinters of glass. No, I would not have liked to be here yesterday. Now everyone is obviously exhausted. The peace of a cemetery prevails. When I turn into Nazimabad, the streets are clear again. Once more I take a sharp turn off the main street and look for a hidden patch through the hills, because a huge cloud of smoke is rising in the main street, possibly the road sweepers are burning the trash, possibly the mob is burning a bus.

You cannot be too sure. When I arrive at the school in Manghopir I have gained another experience: as a rule, things work out fine. This rule seems to apply to Karachi as well. Just do not be afraid. I am glad to have taken the risk when I see Suraya's and Salima's happiness, and their relief that I have come, at least someone has come, even though not the whole community. "It's not that bad, really," I say casually. "Yesterday it was bad, but that is over now."

How do we face the challenge of fighting leprosy in Greater Karachi? "We will have leprosy under control in Pakistan by the year 2000" is the creed of the team, "with the exception of Greater Karachi." Until now, nobody had doubted that it was impossible to wage a systematic battle against leprosy in this city of thirteen million inhabitants. Until February 1995, we had not got together and dared to ask the question aloud that had moved us all secretly for a long time: Is it really unavoidable that leprosy is spreading in this city that is so stricken with other afflictions? In the face of all the violence, we can only help in certain cases, if at all. But maybe we can perform the service of fighting leprosy.

We decided to at least try it.

You have to visualize once again the geography of this city. Its estimated thirteen million inhabitants are distributed in four districts. The riots are more common in those areas where Indian immigrants live: Lalukhet, New Karachi (and especially the part of town called G11), and Korangi–Landhi (a twin satellite town). Riots occur in Malir also, but not as severely as elsewhere. Orangi is the most terrible area. There we started last with our systematic work.

I recall the frustration of earlier years, when we could not reach some patients. Neither the patients dared to leave their residential areas nor the leprosy technicians to drive into the area. Helpless, frustrated, and with a troubled conscience, we would spend the morning hours at the outstation.

Should we have tried to drive in to aid them? Our courage to ask that question aloud was probably the breakthrough in February 1995. We asked aloud, "Is it really as impossible as the authorities believed?" The authorities had aimed to prove that it was impossible, assigning to Karachi the status of "disaster area." If this was correct, we were no longer obliged to get leprosy under control in Karachi.

Yet maybe it was only difficult and not impossible?

And with that, we decided to start working systematically and full of dedication. The old motto of the team was valid: "Dead or alive, we will do this now!"

Where should we start with our attempt? In G11. Why? Because it is especially dangerous there. If we can do it in G11, then we can do it in the whole of Karachi.

Who wants to volunteer?

Morning in G11

We tucked the medical files under our arms and went on our way to New Karachi, to the part of the city called G11, which is the most disreputable block of New Karachi, one of the innumerable satellite towns of this city of thirteen million inhabitants. Two rival terrorist groups are fighting for predominance in this area. They have conquered their territories in bitter street fights, street after street. One of the narrow alleys is ruled by one party, the next street by its opposing party, their enemies. They have built posts out of sandbags and have armed them with machine guns to defend their territory against attackers. These "freedom fighters" are mostly teenagers, fifteen to eighteen years old. Some of the boys are about twenty years old. The inhabitants do not dare leave their houses and therefore do not come for their leprosy treatment.

We leave the car outside G11. The side streets are each guarded by one of the terrorist groups.

"Shall we go on?" I ask.

No vote against.

Holding the medical files demonstratively under our arms, we walk toward the boys behind their barricades, in the direction of the rifles that are pointed at us. I walk in front, as a cover for the team. A woman of my age will not be fired on as easily as a group of young men suspected of carrying weapons.

"Excuse me," I ask them in Urdu, "could you please help us? I am worried about one of my patients. She didn't come to be treated. We have her medication with us but we don't know where she lives."

There is a moment of surprised silence, insecure, aggressive silence.

They look in a hostile way over the two young men who have come with me. My heart is racing. Later, in the car, we tell each other how uneasy we all had felt.

"This is the medical file," I tell them. "Would you like to take a look at it?" One of the armed boys offers me a blue, rickety plastic chair. "Would you like to sit down?" The ice is broken. They grant us an escort. On that day, we take care of all our patients in that area. Everything goes well.

Only once we almost get into the crossfire, when the boys behind the two different sandbag dugouts start shooting at each other. When there is shooting, both sides are ready to continue until they run out of ammunition. We are on the open street, where should we look for cover? All the doors are barricaded.

No, one is open. A young woman rushes out of the house, pulls us through the open door, which she barricades at once after us. Relieved, she drops onto the charpoy. "Thanks be to Allah," she says. "I thought I would be too late."

We do not know each other. No, this is a wrong statement. We *didn't* know each other. In this minute of danger, we got to know each other.

The last case this morning turns out to be the aunt of the ringleader. In the end, we are drinking a bottle of Coke with him, which his aunt has donated. We discuss with the leader our plan that we want to go on with our visits in the area on a monthly basis. It seems as though these young men of the machine-gun generation are glad to do something constructive and useful for once, to be needed for a service that makes sense.

Something else struck me that morning in the district of G11: Salam, the youngest in the group that accompanied me, was a Pathan, someone who grew up with the vendetta code of honor. They had not trusted us completely, these teenage terrorists. One of them had always turned up, here and there, obviously in order to monitor us. When we eventually returned to the car, Salam told this boy who had his machine gun ready to fire, very relaxed, "Are you happy? We are."

Salam had the inner freedom to address the other man as a person, to say, "Was it good for you? For us, this worked out really well." This means, very concretely, that we have the possibility to put a stop to evil, even if only at certain points. If this is done everywhere, changes may come.

In the late afternoon, we were back at the outstation.

"When I heard this morning that G11 was on our schedule, I felt kind of queasy," Mukeem said. "I had a real stomachache."

"Me, too," I said, "really queasy."

We were speaking Urdu, the language of the country.

"And now," I asked him, "how was your day?"

Mukeem laughed and changed into English.

"Super nice!" Mukeem said enthusiastically.

For one heartbeat I was back in Afghanistan, in September 1994, when we were taking stock of the past ten years of our mission in Afghanistan.

"And that is exactly why we are invincible," Hussain said. "Our defenselessness is our strength."

The district of G11 was our trial balloon and the beginning of a change in Karachi. After that, we ventured into all the other districts of this huge city, too.

Soon we were trying our luck in Korangi. We jumped over the trenches and groped our way along the walls into the housing areas. That also went well. Then we tried it in Malir, where we succeeded as well. Then we got together and said, "It is obviously possible. However, our present method of working has to be corrected in two ways. First, we have to distribute the medication at distribution centers that the patients can reach on foot. Bus rides are too risky, since there are too many strike days. Furthermore, the bus is dangerous. If the patients use the bus on their way to the distribution centers, they don't know if they can get a ride back." Consequently, we tied our net of distribution centers tighter. Second, men were never to go on a mission without a woman to accompany them. Since then, there is always a woman on each team. We, of course, used this as a message in favor of the women: "You can't even go on a mission without a woman going ahead of you!"

And that in the patriarchal society of Pakistan!

The Impossible Is Possible

In February 1996 we analyzed the statistics. We were all full of hope and in high spirits. The results had justified our commitment.

We discharged from our treatment as healed 864 patients who had suffered from leprosy. If we managed to heal another 204 patients, we would lower the number of leprosy cases below the critical mark, where the illness would no longer spread as an epidemic. "Good," said Hamid, the leprosy field officer who was responsible for this project. Then he added thoughtfully, "And what we were able to achieve—peace in that area—is even more beautiful."

I learned a lot during that time. I admire the incredible will of these people to survive. During the three months I lived and worked in these slum areas, I could not take one single breath that was not polluted, twenty-four hours a day. It literally stank to high heaven because all the sewers were blocked. Then there was the heat, and it had been raining into the bargain. There was no sewage system for rainwater; all of it collected in the streets. And the mosquitoes! Everything seemed horrible and oppressively hopeless. And still, fathers tried to feed their families under the most adverse of conditions; young people got married; children were born and grew up with incredible imaginations and joy of living. I saw boys on the streets who made for themselves small rifles out of cardboard boxes. When you pulled a lever, they went "pop."

At first I thought, "For heaven's sake, that game should be stopped!" And then I remembered our own children's games during the bombing of Leipzig. We put our dolls into the prams, pushed them around, and tried to get out on the street, checking which doors had not been buried under rubble. We had to do that in order to "play away" our fear. The children of Karachi, who played with their self-made Russian toy guns, obviously had to do that as well.

Behind the noviciate building, there was a grand, big playing field. In the evening the boys met there to practice karate. At first, I thought it would be unsafe for children to be outside at that time of the day. Yet karate is a disciplined way to channel your fear and to test your physical strength.

Life goes on. We pretend that everything is all right. Madness becomes a part of normality. Is it good that we behave normally? I think yes, it is. The alternative would be to go mad oneself.

In his novel *Tides of Silence*, Elie Wiesel tells the story of Michael, who is tortured in order to betray his friend. Eventually he is thrown into a cell together with a lunatic. Michael then tries to take care of the completely petrified, mad young man in his cell. The story remains open-ended. It does not tell you if Michael is successful in getting through to the boy. However, Wiesel's message is this: to *try* is important. That is the last island, the last refuge in order not to go mad.

It is possible to have certain small positive experiences.

I can still see before me the boy who had made himself a small paper ship and let it sail in the sewage water. Each time the ship turned, passing a new stream of sewage, the little one cheered. I thought, "Well, that is another way to look at life."

> Even if it is rarely published by the media, I still believe it: no gesture of understanding, effort for peace, affection, and human warmth, be it ever so small, is lost because there is a chain reaction of good.

Is it possible to change a system for the better by force? I doubt it. However, politics are not made by individuals alone. The individuals are products but also agents of change of their society. How many people had to suffer for their convictions before a man such as Mikhail Gorbachev could rise? If the climate of a society is to be changed, many have to support that process. It is comforting to experience again and again, to experience a hundredfold, that people can prevent injustice in their small area of influence. They can oppose a hundred times the powers of destruction with their inconspicuous and unnoticed yes to life. Even if it is rarely published by the media, I still believe it: no gesture of under-standing, effort for peace, affection, and human warmth, be it ever so small, is lost because there is a chain reaction of good, just as there is a chain reaction of evil.

What can be done, in my small area, to reduce the danger of violence and terror? Maybe I can help the people around me experience happiness. Man is created to be happy. Everyone who has once experienced this difference, that success brought about by force provides thrills while care for others provides true happiness, will be forever hungry for this happiness and immune to the thrills of terrorism.

That is probably just what our employees experience in these opera-tions—happiness. So we will probably always hunger for true happiness because man has a natural inclination for the good, which is identical with true happiness.

And then even the impossible becomes possible: in this city of terror, leprosy is controlled today.

Madness has not triumphed entirely.

15

Peace, Religious Fundamentalism, and Human Rights

Islamic Conviction in Manghopir

How does Islamic fundamentalism express itself in our everyday life?

I remember one morning in Manghopir, at our home for the handicapped. I can still see that old man before me, and also the other excited patients who were desperately trying to prevent him from giving me his message. I could see from afar that they wanted to appease him. He, on the other hand, was adamant: No, no, he had to tell me, no matter what.

Then he stood in front of me and said solemnly, "I am an old man. I am not going to live very much longer. You are such a wonderful woman; I would like to meet you again in heaven. Why can't you become a Muslima?"

I was deeply touched. What should I tell him? That this might be a bit difficult, but that I was sure that God would agree that we meet again in heaven. I assured him that it was the same for me; I would also like to meet him again.

The old man from Manghopir went to heaven long ago, where he is smiling about the remark he made then.

This is a story about fundamentalism that is worth telling. Normally only alarming news is published by the newspapers.

The Fascination of the Easiest Solution

The combination of religion and politics lies in the nature of Islam.

However, the concept of Islam as state religion, or even as theocracy, is not a Pakistani tradition. The founder of the state of Pakistan, Muhammad Ali Jinnah, had demanded a secular state in the 1940s, and had declared at the founding of Pakistan in 1947 that everyone was first of all a Pakistani and only then a Hindu, a Christian, or a Muslim.

Pakistan became "Islamized" under General Muhammad Zia-ul-Haq, a devout Muslim who considered it his duty to introduce Islam in Pakistan. Yet he was not an aggressive fundamentalist. He had an excellent relationship with the Christian minority. He was one of those officers of the British army, educated in Sandhurst, who had adopted much of Western thought.

I cannot imagine a permanent victory of fundamentalism, any fundamentalism, not only the Islamic variety, because a theocracy stands in contrast to historical developments. It is an outdated form of state. Nevertheless, it is alluring at the moment as a simple and radical solution from Peshawar to Texas.

The militant fundamentalist trends have only come to Pakistan in the past ten years. The Saudi-Arabian influence by the Wahhabists has a part in this development.

And there are more.

The unjustified, prolonged American war in Afghanistan with its untold suffering by the civil population, the attack on Iraq—it is these developments to which our Islamist parties owe their landslide victory. It has only been now, in the first months of 2004, that I have spent six weeks in North-West Frontier Province where the Islamist parties formed the provincial government. I was a bit apprehensive—whom would I find in the government chairs? But then it was the same, like it has been for thirty-five years. No change. Sometimes I thought it might even be a bit improved, a new government proving its worth to the people of the province. Occasionally you could hear voices speaking of "appointment by merit," and here and there they even tried and implemented it. It was a new culture but our arguments—that *merit* must be counted and not only seniority—were getting increasingly less strange to them.

Do I think therefore that there is no danger, nothing to be watched out for? This would be an understatement, too. There is a definite upsurge of tribal law, of public executions without formal legal proceedings, the way it was in vogue when I first came to Pakistan. In the meantime, the tribal culture has been increasingly shedding its century-old rough customs, so that actually, in 1995, the jungle law of Karachi surpassed by far the jungle law of our tribal areas. I would no longer uphold this today.

Terrorism is an everyday event: talk among normal citizens, reports in the papers. The terrorists quote Islam as their motive, though there is no theological backing of this interpretation. And from Pervez Musharraf (our chief) to the highest religious authority in Saudi Arabia during Hajj, it is stressed again and again that there is no place for violence in "true" Islam.

So why do they discredit Islam over and over again?

Abuse of women, this too is an old topic that flared up anew or, possibly, it was never overcome. Only these days it is at least getting publicity. Has this caused any changes? Somehow we seemed to get so accustomed to it. This is what worries me most: with such news in the papers this culture can still live.

Recently we were looking at old photos; we are organizing an archive about the history of leprosy in Pakistan. I had to laugh—this young lady doctor with her all-male team in the slum quarters of Orangi. Short skirts and tight trousers—today I would stop any one of our volunteers who ventures out into the street in such as outfit!

Yesterday (March 2004) a girl cycled to school—in Islamabad—and it made headlines in the English paper. In these small events we feel it always again, that we are living in an oppressive society. But mostly we are quite relaxed.

A decisive point for Afghanistan was the appearance of the Taliban. They were students of madrassas, Islamic religious schools, trained in the Wahhabist bases of Pakistan. Suddenly thousands of these students emerged in Afghanistan, bringing back the "true" Islam to this country, from which, they said, the mujahideen had deviated, seeking only power and influence. All these warlords did was kill and loot, the Taliban blamed, but they no longer paid attention to what Islam was really about. The Taliban even confiscated cameras because they regarded them as non-Islamic. Schools for girls were closed. The Taliban, however, were famous for not accepting any bribes. Two-thirds of all Afghanis sided with this group voluntarily. People were just tired of being robbed every other week by another tribal leader. And the Taliban allegedly did not seek political power. But when they came near Kabul and ran up against resistance there, they turned out to be very well equipped militarily and excellently trained with regard to all kinds of weapons. A Taliban can drive a tank and use a machine gun. Supposedly there are even fighter pilots among them—and that is something you do not learn at regular madrassas. So this is the fate of militant fundamentalism: the Taliban has degenerated into one of the many political forces that have only one ideal, to seize power in Afghanistan.

It has never been officially confirmed nor denied by the government that these students of the Qur'an came from Pakistan. However, Afghanistan no longer had an infrastructure at that time. When it finally leaked out that fundamentalist groups were offering complete military training in their Pakistani Islamic schools, the government intervened officially: the Islamic schools and their curricula had to be registered. There was resistance and also turmoil in parliament. A law was passed, but that does not mean much in Pakistan. There are many laws—and good ones, for that matter—but only a few of them are ever implemented

Return to the "True" Islam

There are, however, also positive trends in Pakistan, which are to be counted among the so-called near fundamentalist groups. To return to the "true" Islam has remained a real vision for many. There is, for example, the lay movement called Tabligh. Some of our patients and a few employees belong to it. Ordinary people commit themselves for one to three months to explain the basic rules of Islam to their brothers and sisters in faith. This work is done in groups as a neighborhood mission. They take a vow for this period, among other things, never to lie.

We give the patients who are involved in this movement their medication to take at home. If they say they will take the medication, we can rely on them to really do it because they cannot lie. We talk to the leaders of groups that have leprosy patients among them. The group does not mind having them at all. These people are courageous as well. To speak openly against the cultivation of opium, as they have done, can mean that you are putting your life at risk.

Admittedly, a certain naivety in this Tabligh movement is obvious. There is, for example, the story of Gulab, one of our leprosy technicians.

He is a young man from a very backward mountain area who had gone through an identity crisis and in that situation had come under the influence of drugs. According to his wishes, we placed him in the care of a Tabligh group at that time. They took very good care of him and succeeded in helping him get off drugs and stay clean. So Gulab became deeply connected with this group.

I became an eyewitness of how they help people like him. They do not force themselves upon you; they only offer their religious services. They sit in one of the small tearooms, chat at their ease, visit people at home. Whoever wants to listen can do that, and whoever does not want to is not forced to listen. Everyone is free to say, "I don't want to talk to you." They lack the fanatical force of the rigorous fundamentalists yet they are firm in their will to live the life of the Holy Prophet with all its deprivations. And that is what Gulab was doing at that time, too. He would not sit down on a chair even in a hotel. He squatted on the ground because the Holy Prophet had not had chairs. He only slept on the ground, he only ate on the ground, he kept all the prayer times. In short, he was trying to live the Holy Prophet's life as a Berber in the twentieth century.

Against Fanaticizing

The Pakistani fundamentalist party Sipah-e-Sahaba (SSP) certainly has to be regarded differently from the Tabligh movement. For Tabligh missionaries, the issue really is religion; for the SSP, it is power—religion for them is just a means to an end. It is obvious that people can be stirred to fanaticism through religious demagogy. Susceptibility to fanaticism, to the abuse of religion—you will find this in more than just developing countries. Probably we are all susceptible. This feeling is presumably embedded in deep recesses of the human mind and cannot be so easily and quickly controlled intellectually.

Fundamentalism only really becomes a danger—often this is what makes it possible at all in the first place—when groups are forced into ghettos. Islam as a religion, like Christianity, includes fundamentalism as a possibility. We ourselves are watchful that religious feelings do not grow explosive socially. This is not possible through academic discussion groups alone. We have to meet in the middle, listen to each other. We have to not only do something *for* other people but also *with* them—celebrate with them—in order to search for community in shared commitment.

We can only experience the "other" in his or her own image if we open ourselves up. But the historically strained relations between Islam and Western Christianity make it difficult to start an intellectual conversation between people who do not yet trust and accept each other. Only if you have already encountered the other, if you have made the effort to know somebody, will your interest in him or her grow.

> We have to meet in the middle, listen to each other. We have to not only do something *for* other people but also *with* them—celebrate with them—in order to search for community in shared commitment. We can only experience the "other" in his or her own image if we open ourselves up.

We cannot expect Muslims to feel the need to get closer to Christianity. How they see it, they not only have the truth but they have also included everything that was important in Christianity, after six hundred years. The only chance to arouse interest in a dialogue between the two religions is to arouse interest in each other, to make people curious about each other. When Muslims in Karachi asked us some years ago to explain to them why Christian relief organizations were working successfully and Muslim ones were not, someone from our team organized an afternoon meeting about the topic of incarnation. That was only possible against the background of a request and of mutual interest. If we had planned from the outset to have an event for the purpose of theological information, it would have been interpreted as indoctrination and consequently would have been suppressed or ignored.

1 6

Islam: Religion Versus
Cultural Expressions

A Lack of Knowledge and a Concept of the Enemy

Westerners still suffer from a considerable lack of knowledge about Islam. Who among average Christians knows about the common Abrahamaic roots? Who actually knows that Islam has integrated much of the two parts of the Bible, the Old and the New Testaments, even though some of it derives from apocryphal traditions? Many of us do not even know that Islam is a monotheistic religion, not a pagan one.

We have to detach ourselves from the problematic historical details if we want to form an opinion on Islam. The subjection of women, the slaughtering of sacrificial animals, the Sharia law—Islam cannot be identified only by these. Of course, these aspects have to be seen, too. However, details that are perceived in an isolated way prevent us from seeing the whole picture.

Islam cannot be defined through its legal system. If someone claims that Islam is cruel, he is consolidating concepts of "the enemy." If someone says that Islam has not liberated itself of its historical roots, he says the same thing, but without hatred. I can understand something without endorsing it in its historical appearance. Such an understanding makes it impossible to hate the other person. And if you do not hate, the other person remains important to you.

If someone talks about the potential of aggression in Islam, he should also know from where it is derived. Islam faces the difficulty that it cannot perceive itself as a historical religion because of its self-perception. The Holy Book is the unchangeable eternal revelation. And still Muslims live in an environment that is changing constantly and dramatically. Christianity comprehends itself as historical from its theological concept of incarnation: revelation has *not* been given finally, but appeared in the form of a child, a child like any other, who developed like any other child, learned from his mistakes and experiences, into a young man who had to find his way. In contrast, a Muslim believes in revelation as a written message that is final.

Historical Differences

Because Christianity, not Islam, is a historical religion, Christians are duty-bound to make the first step toward Islam and to understand it in its historical context. Christians must understand it as a religion that is six hundred years younger than Christianity; that has taken many ideas from the New Testament; that has, however, incorporated itself historically in a tribal culture and therefore carries many values of these tribes, values that cannot be explained theologically such as the position of women in Islamic society.

In a sense, it is not fair to compare the Christianity of the year 2003 to the Islam of 2003. We should at least, for a moment, compare the Islam of 2003 with the Christianity of six hundred years ago. In 1403 (and also a little later) we persecuted heretics and believed we were serving God by doing that. And women were subordinate creatures much beyond 1403.

> The only possibility to foster tolerance lies in the
> insight that the absolute truth is always received by a
> fallible intellect … I have to be tolerant because I do
> not know if I have really perceived the absolute truth,
> which transcends my limited understanding. I do not
> know if I have not erred in the perception of the truth.

Truth is absolute. Thus Christianity has to uphold its claim to absoluteness, as does Islam. However, the only possibility to foster tolerance lies in the insight that the absolute truth is always received by a fallible intellect: I am not able to be tolerant with regard to the truth with which I have been entrusted; however, I have to be tolerant because I do not know if I have really perceived the absolute truth, which transcends my limited understanding. I do not know if I have not erred in the perception of the truth. It is an issue of my intellectual credibility to be aware of the limitations of my perception. Therefore, tolerance is also a question of logic.

Tolerance and Intolerance

In the day-to-day coexistence of religions in Pakistan, tolerance has not been achieved yet. In principle, a Muslim who converts to Christianity no longer has any "home." I have seen cases like this, where people have been cast out by their families and not yet accepted by Christians.

When the two daughters of one of our employees, young women with good educations, converted to Christianity, they had to disappear at first for security reasons, until the excitement in their family and neighborhood had died down. But even this experience cannot be generalized. Today, S. and R. live again in the same part of town, work in the education sector, have their own families, and the relations with their family and neighbors are as normal as before.

When D. V. went to Mass in the chapel of our hospital, and everyone knew that he had taken that important step, everybody agreed that he had "always" been a Christian because of his attitude, his ethos as a physician. Around this time, Aziz, a very pious Muslim and longtime employee, came for a short visit from Balochistan. He had not yet heard about the new events and was inquiring after D. V.

"Is it true that he got married?" he asked, obviously disappointed. I laughed, "We were all glad for him," I said. "He already has his first baby daughter. She is only three days old!"

Aziz seemed disturbed, "No, I had always expected him to join an order."

"As a Muslim?" I asked.

"Well, anyway," Aziz told me, "he is so special, he simply belongs in an order."

It is not only Christians who are in danger because of fundamentalism—or not even mainly them. Christians, as followers of a "religion of the Book," enjoy a certain safety granted to minorities. Jews also have a "religion of the Book," however the feeling against Jews is very strong in Pakistan. No wonder—most of the problems we create ourselves. Anyone who has firsthand information about the Israel-Palestine conflict, the constant suppression, the countless hopes, disappointment again and again, knows where this feeling comes from—has to come from. A people not belonging anywhere. Where shall they go? Only this animosity has no consequences in Pakistan, as we have no Jewish communities in the country.

Once, Sultan Mohammed, a leprosy technician in the mountains of the Himalayas, wrote to me after a group of our volunteers had worked there. "I really think it's great that the girls are so devout; they read every morning in their Holy Book. But please tell them—*please* tell them!—to treat it with more respect! I see that they put it in the same compartment of their backpacks as their shoes!" And I did tell the girls!

The Ahmadi are probably the religious group that is most in danger. They embrace all the Muslim doctrines but beyond that, they also believe that Mirza Ghulam Ahmad possessed a special revelation. With this, the Ahmadi are considered a group betraying Islam, as they consider him as a prophet after the last prophet.

The Hindus are also in a very precarious situation; they are "idolaters." It is not unusual in Pakistan to discuss the question whether they really have a soul or not, if they do not believe in the one God. And if they do not have one, what should prevent us from eliminating them if need be?

What Is It That Connects Us?

The fact that the debate about the universality of human rights is going on all over the world shows us that the issue of human rights addresses something important. I am convinced that there are basic feelings that are shared by all people. I remember a lesson at the leprosy technicians' course: among the students, there was no one who had ever had a lesson about human rights. Our last topic had been that the only way to pass on the infection of leprosy was from person to person, so there is really only one sure method to quickly exterminate leprosy: to eliminate the source of the infection.

Therefore the question was asked, "Why don't we just shoot every leprosy patient?" The students protested loudly, "You can't do that!" It is by all means an option in this country to shoot someone. We have in Pakistan, after all, arbitrary law, vendetta, and political murder. But to say to a group, "You carry an infection, therefore, away with you!"—that is obviously impossible, as far as the elementary consensus goes. After that, we discussed the case of an antisocial leprosy patient who was very aggressive. Could we not shoot him at least? Everyone agreed that that was also out of the question. Why? Why! There really could not be any doubt: God, and God alone, is able to "make" man and therefore something is in men that is beyond our "right of disposal."

Of course, we have observed that people in Pakistan were excluded from their community for various reasons. That entails weighing priorities and values by the tribe. If the existence of the individual threatens the honor of the tribe, then the person might have to die, be he or she leprous or not. Also, when a mother has an illegitimate child, then mother and child are less important than the honor of the clan. However, in principle, the conviction prevails that you cannot simply kill someone because of his or her illness, not even when he acquired leprosy. You only can shun him for various reasons—to stop the spread of infection, or, more common, to shun him as a sinner. This is because in the beginning, and occasionally even today, there is a conviction that leprosy is not an ordinary disease but a curse of God for sins committed in the past.

All of us are born with the concept of "natural rights," or rights according to our natures as members of the human species. These are basic convictions, comprehensible to everyone, without explanation. Therefore, human rights have to be an issue wherever people live together. Though if laws are to develop from this, and if concrete cases for their use come up, misunderstandings are bound to occur. What is it that connects us all around the world? What are the human rights of an individual? What is the role of the group with regard to the individual? When we deal with these questions we are ruled by different convictions. Who can tell whom what is right, what is wrong?

These are difficult problems that raise questions not only for Pakistan but also for Western societies. What are the rights of the individual with regard to the community? I do not think that individual rights should be abrogated. Rather, they should be supplemented by duties. I cannot insist on these rights if I do not feel bound to the community.

Not even Western society can exist as a collection of individuals. You realize that whenever there is ice on the streets, people can prevent slipping and falling down only if they support each other. When I talk about my work in Germany, I use the word "we" most of the time. Then I am asked who is behind that "we." It is difficult to say "I," simply because in the morning, someone has already prepared the breakfast I eat, because the clothes that I wear have been made by someone else, and because the staircase that I walk down has been built by someone else. The "I" only exists on the basis of the "we."

> It is difficult to say "I," simply because in the morning, someone has already prepared the breakfast I eat, because the clothes that I wear have been made by someone else, and because the staircase that I walk down has been built by someone else. The "I" only exists on the basis of the "we."

In the West, we have to learn again something that in Pakistan is still a natural experience. If you cross a mountain river in the Himalayas, you never go alone. If you slip on the stones, you will be carried away by the torrent. Therefore, it is an unwritten law that three people take each other by the hand and so fight their way across the torrent. Three people do not fall at the same time. If one of them stumbles, the other two will stand and hold him. If the other one slips then the first one will be on his feet again. That is the only chance to reach the other bank.

If people have liberated themselves, they should take a look around and ask themselves, and what about this newly won freedom? We should give away so much of our own freedom voluntarily that it fits into the context of the people around us, without unsettling them.

"Your Freedom Ends Where My Nose Begins"

"*Azadi*—freedom." The fascination of every psychology lecture has to do with levels of human freedom.

Take Abraham Maslow's hierarchy of needs. On the lowest level are the basic needs such as nourishment, clothing, security. Above those are social needs: friendship, recognition. And the highest level includes self-realization and freedom.

"And what happens when my social needs run into conflict with the security needs of someone else?" Salma wants to know.

Why?

The material is still too new for the group to be able to get into it. Salma defends herself, "Finally I can imagine the case that, on my son's birthday, I would like to be home. And just on that very day, there is perhaps no co-worker in the outpatient station. So then the patients can't be properly attended to."

The group is puzzled; no reaction, quiet.

Until Ashraf comes to speak. "That will frequently occur," he says unmoved, "but then there is simply only one way. You must go into the highest story of the pyramid, activate your freedom, and say 'I'm going anyway, voluntarily.'"

"Do you know the story about the country that received its freedom?" Khadim picks the thread up. The people danced and celebrated in the streets. And they tossed their firearms over their heads. And one of them hit the nose of a mountain farmer.

> I have discovered a key idea of our work in the Urdu language, which is used by many in Pakistan as the *lingua franca*. The concept of *apnana* means "both of us, you and I, simultaneously make the reality of the other our own."

"'Hey', he said, 'what are you doing?'"

"'Celebrating my freedom,' the man with the firearm said. And the farmer replied, 'Listen, your freedom stops where my nose begins.'"

That became the household expression of the team, "Your freedom ends where my nose begins."

We find our fulfillment and our limit with the other. Your freedom stops at my nose. Your freedom stops here in my uniqueness.

I have discovered a key idea of our work in the Urdu language, which is used by many in Pakistan as the *lingua franca*. The concept of *apnana* means "both of us, you and I, simultaneously make the reality of the other our own."

This is the way that leads further.

This way includes dialogue and peaceful coexistence with the other.

17

Among Muslims

Life According to My Convictions

Countries such as Afghanistan and parts of Pakistan are still almost archaic. The methods of the police are also relics of brute tribal orders.

In order to change that, it is not enough to demonize individuals as "bloodhounds." The whole country must change; mentalities that have deep roots in general behavioral structures have to be changed. But in the meantime, in a country where fathers slay their children with an axe when they suspect extramarital relations, and where people accept this, I certainly cannot claim my own Western ideals as the norm.

Of course, as a woman who belongs to a religious order and is conditioned by Western thought, I live in a situation full of conflicts. But can I and should I expect that this Muslim country is going to follow my ideals of a Western order? Should I go home because it does not? My task, as I see it, is to try to live my convictions and let myself be asked these questions again and again: "Why are you doing this? Why do you behave differently?"

I have found that my work has been accepted and somehow, by osmosis, helped one or the other to redefine, or just find, his or her ideals, too.

The Sharia

The day after General Zia successfully staged a coup in Pakistan, he called a man I had been a friend with for years, a well-known lawyer, a devout Muslim, a faithful supporter of MALC, who was also known as a spiritual leader. The general said, "I have observed again and again that people who come to power lose the right way. Are you ready to become my spiritual guide?" This friend went to Islamabad, and later became the minister of justice.

I did not visit him during that time, and deliberately did not continue our regular exchange of thoughts. Later, when he had left the office, he reproached me for that. He said, "In the most difficult time, when I really needed you, you did not come to me." I had, indeed, been to his house in Islamabad five times and had returned home without ever ringing the bell. The Islamic legal system was so problematic for me that I could not bring myself to meet him. But was that right?

Through this friend I had the opportunity to get to know the general personally. Our first subject was the value of intercession. When the Islamic penal system was introduced, I asked the general if he was not afraid that this kind of a legal system could poison the atmosphere in the country, even down to the families. The tenor of his answer was, "Who am I, General Zia, that I should question something that is inscribed and clear in the Islamic system?"

This is a conflict we have to live with. Islam and Christianity are two monotheistic religions with a similar claim to revealed truth.

How can we then live as brothers and sisters? Truth is entrusted to us; we cannot betray it. But the perception of *truth*, the full perception of truth, for this our human mind is not made. We are too small for the unbelievable gift made to us. We only perceive parts of the truth. So we have to give the right to the other to see his truth, this eternal precious truth from a different angle. We will not ever solve this question of final truth.

> We are too small for the unbelievable gift made
> to us. We only perceive parts of the truth. So we
> have to give the right to the other to see his truth,
> this eternal precious truth from a different angle.

Then, what is our task on earth? To *live* this brotherhood, this sisterhood in love and understanding.

The Sharia—nothing is as confusing for me and as disturbing as the Pakistani legal scene. A number of legal systems seem to coexist, cross, refute one another, and they all seem to be in force. Once I asked the German ambassador, a real friend of mine, to explain it to me, what it is all about. He smiled. "Don't try to understand it," he said. "I don't understand it either. Nobody understands it."

Yet common people are the victims of this nonfunctioning, confusing system.

I do have experience with the legal system—the brute force, exercised in the police stations, the lower courts, where it normally counts who knows whom, and who pays how much—and the High Court, where you have hope that you will get justice after long, long months and years of waiting and at considerable cost, but you do get justice, and for this we are grateful.

Then there is still the street law, the tribal law, the family law—all rooted in tradition and therefore so strong. *Karo Kari*, the honor killing of a woman, a man under suspicion of infidelity, is not yet recognized as murder. Acid throwing—dousing a woman with kerosene, putting a match to her, and saying the cooking stove exploded—I know but one single case where the perpetrator was sentenced. Honor killings are not murder cases; it is a "gentleman's offense," and we all know what motives are often behind these killings!

There is not a week that we do not deal with a human rights case among our own patients, our employees. Ruzy, we got free. He had been accused and convicted of an illegal relationship with a girl. All lies. Salam was released on bail last week. He has been in jail for two years after he was caught with heroin in his luggage. The man who used him as a carrier—they mostly use minors, even girls—got off scot-free. It is not possible to argue a case in detail, or at least it is very, very difficult. One of the patients in Quetta was accused of murder and convicted. A tribal chief had taken advantage of a defenseless Afghan refugee who, in addition, was suffering from leprosy—and this was his luck. We got him out. There was no possibility to sue the state, the accuser, for compensation. Four people were convicted in connection with a Christian boy who had eloped with a Muslim girl. Two we got free, two are still in jail, a notorious jail for that matter. The case has reached the High Court in Islamabad. We paid the lawyer, and after ten months we are still waiting for the date of hearing. Why is it not set? I do not know. Another one of our employees has been out on bail for four years. The case does not move, though legally it is a clear case, no evidence ever produced. I do not know how much of my savings is frozen in bail to get people out of jail, people who would otherwise spend years of their lives in confinement, their families suffering seriously.

This is only a rough summary of our own cases, where people often hesitate to get involved because they know we shall not sit back and let it happen. What about all the others? Nevertheless, this is not all.

There are courageous human rights groups. Friends we can call on. Women's groups who speak up. Laws have been repealed, after long struggles, that now give equal rights to minorities in the election of the country. I know what I am talking about; I have followed their struggle. It is not without risks. Activists have paid their convictions with their lives as sacrifice.

"Dialogue" Means to Expose Oneself

We must learn to find true access to one another. To study is not enough for that. A change of heart is required, a love that accepts the other person, exposes itself to him or her. This is a kind of love that also has to do with sacrifice. What a painful process it is, what an act of dying already, if someone wants to divest himself of his cultural heritage. In the beginning, I believed that my decision to go to Pakistan would mean a total break with my old life, the final leap, and a complete identification shift. But my European identity reaches much deeper than I had ever thought.

> We must learn to find true access to one another.
> To study is not enough for that. A change of heart
> is required, a love that accepts the other person

To really let oneself be broken open, to let the other person enter with all his differences and to welcome him, that is very difficult and even dangerous. There will always be a rest that refuses itself. Or does it thereby preserve itself? That has to resist in order to preserve itself! Just as love between a man and a woman is not about conformity but about devotion in tension, so is a real encounter between cultures, between religions. It is only possible for us to give something to each other because we are different. However, we also suffer from each other because we are different.

But there is not only suffering. There is also fascination and mutual gain. There is the interest of my Muslim partners, too. During my first

years in Pakistan, when I went to a government office to make a request,
to gain an import permit or a residence permit, I encountered a likely situation. The official glanced at me and asked, "Are you Dr. Pfau?" When
I said yes, he inquired, "Is it true that you have taken a vow of chastity?"
He was fascinated by the fact that revelation could so determine one's
life, could be so unquestioningly real, that one would sacrifice "the most
beautiful thing in the world"—to have children—light-heartedly.

Ecumenical Differences

Difficulties occurred when things became concrete. Our leprosy technicians found themselves in a real identity conflict at the time of the
armed conflict with Bangladesh. It was, after all, a war in which Muslims fought against Muslims. I implored my Muslim lawyer friend,
"You must help them. You must do something for them. I cannot argue
within your own system that I could comfort them." But he was unable
to commit himself to that, not to a social group for which he would
have had to find a new language. Even though he admires social commitment, he is unable to do it himself.

This kind of religious conversation had been going on for years
between us. I told my friend that after we have been on the way together
for such a long time, we should initiate a shared prayer group. To lead
the dialogue spiritually, not apologetically, is a way that surely points
to the future. There are central starting points in both religions. We
ultimately did not succeed but that we can pray together is now a long
tradition in the program. There is no opening of a workshop, no celebration, no feast of any one of the religious groups that we would not start
with a common prayer. The recitation of the Holy Qur'an comes first;
we cover our heads with scarfs (whenever we wear one). Then comes
the reading from the Holy Bible, or a spontaneous Christian prayer.
And finally one of the Hindus recites from the Gita. Only then can the
speeches start and the tea be served. We would be missing something if
one was left out.

There is indeed much we discovered to be our common heritage.

Recently, for example, I read some passages to my sister in religion,
Jeannine, and asked her from which gospel they derived. She told me
the exact verses, but she erred. I had quoted from the Holy Qur'an.

There are also difficulties in our ecumenical conversation, such as when the historical approach is taken. That is also a subject I cannot talk about with my Muslim friend. When I start, "Islam is, after all, a historical religion, that emerged in a Berber tribe in the desert at a certain time, so it must have historical wrappings"—he does not see that.

There have been attempts, long ago, to promote the historical approach in Islam in a Muslim Research Institute. The director of this institute, who had also worked for our Muslim-Christian study group, left Pakistan and now teaches somewhere in the United States. He said, "I am understood better in the Roman Catholic office for non-Christians than among my own brothers in the faith."

The Power of Forgiveness

The deepest message Christians owe to Muslims in countries such as Pakistan is the creative value of forgiveness. I believe that, basically, this value is not even necessarily alien to my Muslim friends and co-workers.

There is the story about Jehangir, a leprosy technician, who came from an area where the code of vendetta was part of everyday life. I have traveled with him many times. Due to the lack of infrastructure, you can never be sure if you will return from missions into the mountains. Naturally, this produces a strong team spirit. After one mission, we drove back to the outpatient station, where I had to write my report.

We stayed there for three days. In the morning, I usually meditate by reading in the Bible or the New Testament in Urdu. Urdu is written from right to left, and it has no short vowels. Therefore, you have to know what you are reading before you are able to pronounce it. When I read the New Testament in Urdu, I kill two birds with one stone: I meditate and I practice my Urdu. Incidentally, I had left the book open on my desk. Jehangir found it and got stuck at the Sermon on the Mount. On impulse, completely against Muslim customs, he threw the book on the desk and said, "So this is how you want to oblige us to live!" "For heaven's sake," I said. "First of all, I have never talked to you about the Sermon on the Mount and, secondly, I have never obliged you to follow anything." He never came back to this subject. Jehangir then went on vacation and returned to the team a month later. We asked him how his vacation had been.

"Wonderful," he said.

"And what had been so wonderful about it?" We were understandably curious.

"When I returned to my village, I met someone who told me, 'Listen, I met Mohammad Aslar today and he told me that Jehangir was coming back today. Since Aslar has no sons, I was to be his avenger, because he still has a score to settle with you. The act of revenge has fallen on me.'" After all, he was the nephew of the man who had been offended.

Jehangir went on, "I was racking my brain to remember which score had not been settled between Mohammad Aslar and me. Finally, it came back to me. When I was still at school, I had once knocked him down in the bazaar. Then, I was the hero and he had to clear off. The only son of this man died in an accident in the mountains. He himself was an agricultural laborer without land of his own. So I went over to Mohammad Aslar and told him, 'Here I am, beat me like I beat you then.' Mohammad Aslar was stunned. 'How can I beat you?' But I clarified, 'That is what I came for. You beat me like I beat you, and then we are even.' Mohammad Aslar repeated, 'But how can I beat you? I can't beat you.' And I said, 'Then forgive me.' And he said, 'I do forgive you.' That was a wonderful vacation, a *wonderful* vacation."

The Raid on Gilgit

It was in 1995, a day like any other. We had planned a further education event for a weekend in September in Gilgit Hospital. Northern Areas is more of a small province in the high mountain region, so there were not many workers—fourteen in all, twelve leprosy assistants.

Ampheri, the village at the edge of the town of Gilgit where our hospital is situated, has always been famous for its beauty and, for the last decade, increasingly notorious for its gunfights. It is a bloody ritual; regularly, always at the same time of the year, gunfights flare up between Sunnis and Shia. It is not by chance that this area stands under military administration.

The day has begun. The group is working with great enthusiasm. Yesterday they had a preliminary examination of their tuberculosis patients in the ward and now they introduce their patients. Once again I enjoy the ideal teaching and learning situation. Every sentence is considered to be extremely important for one's own work and therefore taken in with expectant attention.

Rehman accompanied his patients to the hospital. "The children have been sent home from school," he says when he returns. "There's something brewing."

"We ought to get away," Mujib says nervously. Mujib, of all people, the giant from the most belligerent tribe of the province.

"Run away?" I say. "If we interrupt our work at every rumor then soon we won't be able to do anything. They won't come to the hospital."

There is no further argument.

We carry on.

At 11 a.m., tea break, I stay behind in order to prepare the next lesson. They will bring me my tea.

Then suddenly, noise. Something is going on. I run out of the room. A boy with a submachine gun rushes past me. He is good-looking, with fair skin and blue eyes, no older than twenty-two. He puts his foot against the kitchen door, stands in the middle of the room, and shouts—but what? Unarticulated, or in a language that I do not understand. I can still see them, the leprosy assistants, like hens on a perch, directly in front of him, both hands clutching their tea mugs, in front of the muzzle of the Kalashnikov. A volley, and he would have mown them all down.

No, I cannot remember getting hold of him, only that I threw myself between the boys and the machine gun, with spread-out chador—the veil of the Muslim women, the symbol of the mother in his culture, the protecting cloak of the Madonna in mine.

The leprosy assistants take advantage of the situation and disappear like lightning through the open window, outside and into safety. Around the hospital the corn is taller than a man. It offers impenetrable hiding. Only Rashid remains. He was never one for running away. He stays with me and the sick—the ward is full of patients.

The situation gets worse through the flight of the others. The conflict is clear just from observing skin color. Rashid is dark-skinned, clearly recognizable to everyone as a Sunni; the attacker has fair skin, so clearly a Shiite. However, these are not two religions fighting against each other here, they are two enemy tribes.

The seven or ten minutes that pass are an eternity. It is a chase between hunter and prey. A hunt.

I have my chador in front of the machine gun. He aims at Rashid. He runs away, the other follows.

I follow, throw myself between them. The hunt starts anew. Time seems to stand still.

No, the boy is no professional murderer, otherwise he would have shot me long ago. Who puts weapons in the hands of these mountain farmer boys? Who applies pressure to murder? Who forces them to betray their souls? His eyes—I will never forget his eyes. Is it fanaticism? Is that what goes on in the concentration camps and torture rooms all over the world? Hatred—simple, cold, bloodthirsty hatred, which no word and no plea can reach anymore. I try to talk to him. I do not succeed, I cannot reach him. I try again in a reassuring tone of voice, "Tell me who you are looking for on this ward. You can't possibly have come to attack our patients."

I cannot break through the wall between us. "You know that these are my leprosy assistants and over there my patients. You surely can't have come here to shoot dead sick people and leprosy assistants!"

There is not a word for an answer. He is not under the influence of drugs, I would have recognized that, but from his eyes I can see that the boy is simply "not here."

How long will he keep up the cat-and-mouse game? When will the fuse blow? Somehow, through a clumsy movement, I suddenly run straight in front of the submachine gun. No, he did not hit me, but I got so close to him that I hurt myself.

I am bleeding.

At that moment, suddenly a second, much older man appears in the hall, a pistol in his hand. He speaks to me. No, he would not shoot at the patients, he says. Then he disappears again. I am still busy protecting Rashid from the bullets.

The older man comes back, whispers something to the younger one. Perhaps the military has turned up? I summon up hope.

But the older man has only discovered a locked toilet door. Two of our employees have locked themselves in there, and with them three patients who are being cared for on the ward.

When the two employees noticed the attack, they looked for protection in the toilet and locked the room from the inside. If I had known, I would have prevented it. In the meantime, I know the mechanism of such attacks, but it is too late now.

In the hall stood one of our heavy iron beds. Just next to it is the toilet door. The boy with the Kalashnikov, directed by the older man like a puppet, has taken position exactly between the iron bed and the toilet door. I cannot get between them anymore. I beg him, try to hold him back. But my effort is vain. He pushes me away in such a brutal way that I stumble. Then the elder man gets hold of me and hurls me into the corner. When I hit the iron frame, my arm breaks. For a moment I lose consciousness.

By the time I come around again, it is all over. At close quarters they have sieved the wooden door with their bullets, kicked against it with all their might. They have shot down five people in a hail of bullets and have run away and taken flight, although no one was following them.

I struggle to my feet, stumble to the door. Five bodies covered with blood, two dead immediately, two still moaning. The first had fallen over the others and held off the bullets. The youngest of the badly injured, a fourteen-year-old boy, is wearing the pajamas of the inpatients.

I stagger outside, shout across the empty square whether there is anyone who can help. Dead silence.

Suddenly the night watchman appears. "We have to look for the driver," I say, "with my broken arm I cannot steer the heavy vehicle." He holds me back and says, "You can't leave the hospital, the cornfields are full of armed men."

In the distance, the sound of machine gunfire.

It would be stupid to treat the wounded with our means. We would only be losing time. Twenty minutes away is the military hospital, excellently equipped. It is their only chance.

When he hears my voice on the path, Iqbal comes out of hiding. "I will drive, Doctor," he says, "on one condition—that you organize military protection."

At that moment a military patrol is patrolling the upper road. We pant up the hill and stop the soldiers.

The officer posts three of his men. "Run," I say to Iqbal. "I will come after you slowly." Now that the most urgent things have been dealt with, I realize the pain I have. Up to now I have only reacted automatically.

When we reach the outer station again, they are already loading the seriously wounded into the jeep. We drive along the bumpy stone road.

The wounded moan. Outside the shooting has stopped. We will take care of the dead later.

Colonel Farooq is waiting for us in the military hospital. He admits all patients to his wards.

The wounded got their first treatment. While the medical efforts in the operating theater were working to full capacity, I drove back. The other patients and the employees with their families had to be brought in safety. We then ate the lunch that had been cooked before the attack. I insisted on that, even though no one was in the mood for it. "You don't know what we still have to go through; with food in your stomachs you will hold out better." This is a lesson I learned during the air raids in World War II.

During the meal one after the other returns; the high corn had given protection to them all up to now.

On the day after the attack I can at last have an x-ray made of my broken arm. We put on a temporary cast. We are all much too busy to pay further attention to it.

Our employee Ziarat was causing us a lot of worry; he had been shot in his stomach. We fought for his life for a whole week. He was operated on three times, then he had a paralysis of the intestines. Shortly after that he died in the military hospital.

The attack had cost three lives.

But bad luck sometimes brings a ray of hope. A phone call: Ayub, one of our leprosy assistants, had been pulled out of the river two kilometers (one and a quarter miles) below Ampheri, with hypothermia and complete exhaustion. He had been taken to the military hospital. When he heard the shots, he did not know whether his friends were still alive or not. The river seemed to be his only rescue. As he is a good swimmer, he jumped into the water. Wrapped in wool blankets, given an infusion, he later said to me with a weak smile, " I hadn't expected it to be so ice-cold. And the current was much stronger than I had thought."

"Your guardian angel was with you," I said.

And Ayub said in a low voice, "I knew that my mother was praying for me."

Colonel Farooq, the commander of the local garrison, had gone far beyond his official duties to take care of the injured with determination and great helpfulness. The behavior of our team in this extreme situation had clearly made a deep impression on him. As a guest in his home I had the opportunity to exchange thoughts with him and his wife about, above all, honor, vendetta, family honor and revenge, triumph, guilt, revenge and forgiveness.

We were sitting at our evening meal when the police phoned: I was needed for questioning. They had arrested a young man who came into question as being the offender. I ought to identify him. I can still remember how I was filled with panic. But I wanted to talk to the boy. I wanted to ask him, why did you do that? It is difficult for me to live with it—how will you live with it? I wanted to talk to him, but I could not send him to the gallows. We have lost three people. If now a fourth were hanged, it would not bring any of the others back to life. I hid my head in my hands. "I can't," I said in tears, "tell them I can't …"

Colonel Farooq was shocked. He walked to the phone. "I don't understand her either," he said. "She should have been looking forward to this hour of her revenge! But she is different from us, you have to believe her … Yes, I know she is the only eyewitness … but she won't do it because she can't do it."

Farooq hung up, sat down at the table again, and asked, "But why can't you?" The conversation continued until late at night. Forgiveness—so far from Muslim culture and yet virtue is what this country is longing for most. When he walked me through the garden to my room, we stood still for a moment beneath the clear, starry sky.

"About forgiveness," Farooq said suddenly, "why doesn't anyone tell us that? It is a matter of survival for Pakistan that we discover that only forgiveness opens new ways into the future. Three men had to die so that I could learn of it!"

Hassan Ali, the man responsible for the whole leprosy hospital, had in the meantime returned from a further training course. He is a Shiite, like the attackers, and of course he knew the boy who had shot.

Hassan Ali and I were in agreement that we had to speak to the sons of the murdered Ziarat. They still lived in the village. The frontier between the districts of the Shiites and Sunnites runs through the middle of this village.

"The fact that I didn't identify the offender," I said to them, "doesn't mean that you are also obliged not to do it." However, I tried to explain that if we set a chain of revenge and retaliating revenge into motion, our leprosy team would also be endangered. They were all there. Perhaps it ought to be better to make a new start, and that meant forgiveness. It was not hard for me to plead in this way because I was convinced that the boy really was not responsible for his actions. That was no murder; somebody had completely fanaticized him. They accepted that.

The fact that these two young men between twenty and thirty actually renounced the blood vendetta, which for them is a question of tribal honor, was more than I would have dared to hope for in my wildest dreams. The fact that they renounced revenge was one of the great gifts during my time in Pakistan.

18

The Challenge of Growing Old

What Comes After Me?

I had intended to do a great deal of living during my senior years. I wanted to become more involved in human rights activities. I wanted, together with Jeannine and two of our younger sisters, to live on the periphery of society, in a community where anyone who has fallen through the social net could come and not be questioned, where he or she would get a new chance.

We wanted to separate this new beginning, in an organizational sense, from Marie Adelaide Leprosy Center. But our colleagues reacted with panic.

So I have put that aside for the present.

For now, I will continue in the Pakistani-Afghani leprosy project and will gradually prepare for my withdrawal. What will come after me?

The project will not die with me. It will go on. There will be crises but then it will continue onward. There are enough qualified Pakistani workers for when I am no longer available.

I have turned MALC over to my Pakistani management team. This was not done overnight.

Again and again, confidence-building measures are required. Again and again, you need the readiness to solve crises patiently and constructively.

Transfer into local hands is a question of trust. It does not have anything to do with rosy thinking but rather with the readiness to risk. I have very seldom, if at all, experienced any person betray the trust placed in him.

The team has developed its potential. This is the secret of our success. We have trusted them with all our hearts, and the team members did not disappoint our trust.

Our successors do not have the advantage of my initial naivete. They know what normally occurs in Pakistan. They do not expect the extraordinary but rather the normal. And therefore, in all probability, the normal will occur.

As long as we religious sisters were responsible for the project, there were no role models of practical business and consumer management. We sisters did not have any expectations about keeping a customary

Dr. Pfau, on the balcony of Marie Adelaide Leprosy Center, Karachi, in 2004. Photo: DAHW, Harald Meyer-Porzky

material standard of living. We did not need to make careers for ourselves or support a family. We quickly put into effect the social principles of our project. The leprosy technicians had a good time establishing my social profile, grinning as they declared me a typical social case: "She lives below the established living standard in every category for her profession and life as a doctor."

A transfer obviously means that the leprosy project will be in the hands of Pakistanis and so will have to meet the expectations of normal Pakistani officers.

Promotions in Pakistan are primarily viewed not as an increase in duties but as an increase in rights. Yesterday (March 2004) I had to intervene personally. A newly appointed director of health services, responsible for the entire province, declared he was moving into our staff house with his family at 1 p.m. the next day, and if we did not vacate it he would have it vacated by force. The building was constructed with our money. It is the headquarters of the leprosy program of the province, which serves the government. One of our workers was staying in the flat. I left no doubt on what I thought. I could not convince him. But he promised to comply with my wishes. Let's see how the cooperation will develop! This is typical. Therefore I am always delighted to see the many small indications that our "c. i.," our corporate identity, is different. Top management respects the human dignity of even the smallest worker. Our director of administration still today comes with his motorcycle, has no air conditioner in his room—little wonder that he has no difficulties gaining the support of the group in our proposed austerity measures. It is countercultural, but it has become *their* culture.

M.L. tries to formulate it like that: "We have been too deeply influenced by our common values," he says, "we can't, we really are unable to shed it any longer."

There will be a painful but fruitful tension that remains. The identity of the project is not lost thereby. There must be conflicts. West and East are in productive relationship with each other and against each other and for each other. It is a matter of preserving the positive of the Eastern culture in human affections, in family contexts, in the carefree feeling of living life for today.

And what should we take in from Western values? This is the question that is haunting me these days.

I thought I still should empower the group to apply for an international grant, since we need the money—we desperately need it—and the program, which now includes tuberculosis and blindness control, is worthy of sponsorship. I just now had a really good look at the work in the North-West Frontier Province; I criss-crossed the province, amidst rains and snow and fog and *cold*.

We worked hard to produce a document worthy of its name. It included quality control. And then they did not accept it. Reason: "We do not have the mandate for quality control." This is exactly what the colleagues in the government had asked me. They had expanded so fast, they said, that they sacrificed quantity to quality. I loved them for this statement. It is so rare in Pakistan. And it was so true! They did a remarkable job—in their right. You cannot do everything at once. So we were here not to start our own program but to help the program that was already under way.

When you do not treat tuberculosis patients regularly, you not only risk treatment failure but also the danger of resistance. Once the bacteria no longer respond to standard drugs, the treatment gets literally unaffordable. Even if we somehow get the money together, 50 percent of the patients will nevertheless die. In such a way we had converted a curable disease into an incurable one.

I have followed this in Mardan. The district tuberculosis officer was delighted that our team joined his efforts. Together we converted the 56 percent absentee rate into 21 percent then 0 percent. All patients were taking their tablets regularly. We thought we should do this all over. And then this decision: "We have to see that we cover the remaining parts of the provinces." Fine. And, "We can't afford quality control." No mandate for quality control. I had to ask twice before I believed.

Does our Western achievement society know what they are forcing on us? I did not know if I should scream or cry.

I know the Pakistani culture deeply enough. For us, the individual still stands in the center of concern. But the money! The money we get under the conditions of the Western achievement society. Figures count. But who takes the trouble to find out how reliable these figures are? Where are the loopholes? Are the figures tampered with? This is the way people have been surviving for decades and centuries—reporting what the bosses want to know. We act as if we changed that overnight. Why do we not speak up?

Or, if indeed the figures are not tampered with (it would be too good to be true, but who knows, I have seen miracles happen) and are indeed correct, and we know the vulnerability of our culture, why do we not prove that they are correct?

This makes me sick! We had offered quality control; we knew the base for decades. We had offered comprehensive tuberculosis care. We did not want to hunt bacteria, we wanted to cure people—why did they not let us give it a try?

We shall do it nevertheless, simply because otherwise we cannot work. But who will pay for it? This I do not know. Not yet. But still I trust. I trust. There must be money around to do what is right.

Whoever Has No Unshed Tears Cannot Travel This Road

Our future work can only be carried out if the people involved commit to it wholeheartedly and participate fully. Whoever does not carry tears that are ready to flow cannot travel this road. Vulnerability, readiness, and the courage to let oneself be touched—all these are preconditions to become a real leprosy worker. That applies not only to our project and not only to Pakistan.

> Whoever does not carry tears that are ready to flow cannot travel this road. Vulnerability, readiness, and the courage to let oneself be touched—all these are preconditions to become a real leprosy worker.

When we visited Mainz and Germany's chancellor Helmut Kohl, who in the 1970s was minister president of Rhineland-Palatinate, we discussed precisely that issue. He told a story. "When I was prime minister," he said, "the polio vaccinations came up. We delayed acting until I learned that my nephew had contracted polio. Within the next two weeks, polio vaccination was compulsory throughout the province of Rhineland-Palatinate." Kohl continued, "And still today I think to myself, 'That's the way it is. You have to have your own nephew become sick before you really let potential danger for others touch you.' On that day I swore to myself to never give up direct contact with the normal citizen."

There is still so much to do. The point to be emphasized in the present situation of transition is that we have to clarify perspectives. Continuity exists for me in experimenting, in deviating from what "everyone does." For the point that, for example, under some circumstances one hires someone for a project who does not have the required formal qualifications, simply because something must be done and no one else is doing anything. The risk remains. But we take risks consciously and with our eyes open.

> You will never experience happiness if you resist life.
> Happiness can only be experienced with a yes.

You cannot plan life. Life is, by definition, unpredictable.

I have, of late, done a lot of thinking about growing old in an Asian context, and I am still busy with it.

When I turned sixty-five, I packed my suitcases and moved out of the hospital. Why? That is the culture of my country. At sixty-five, you give your place to your successor and you do not interfere in how he wants to run the affairs.

In Asia, your presence is still wanted. Just your presence. The *buzurg*, the "elder," will give stability to the program.

I am still learning my new role.

Who knows what will come?

Roads Not Yet Traveled

And then I would really like to do what Jeannine has already done and what I so often have had to put on the back burner in my life: I would like once again to lead the crazy, adventuresome, and delightfully experimental life of a nun!

That could open up entirely new dimensions in my life, a call to new shores where the roads have not yet been traveled. And this may include illness, age, and loneliness.

I should really get serious about the challenges of growing old. Why? Because I have so intensively tasted all the previous periods that it can bring me something new in my life. Old age is an experience that I do not yet know. No, I cannot agree to "giving up."

Growing old for me does not mean limitation or reduction. That is of no value. I believe that happiness is programmed in life, not impoverishment. Therefore, limitation is always a sign that we have missed a possibility that we are looking at what life offers from the wrong perspective, that we are running after the wrong goal.

So if growing old is on my agenda, and if I do not want to miss this new experience, then it should be lived with all possible intensity. If I do not turn myself toward this new event, if I still hold tight to all the tasks relating to the time of my greatest energy and cling to that, from where will I have the time and the attentiveness to taste these new experiences?

You will never experience happiness if you resist life. Happiness can only be experienced with a "yes."

I have a new yes. "To die in my boots," that is what I previously wished. Today I think otherwise. Departures beckon new ways to the inside, which I have not yet traveled and I do not know where they lead.

It always annoyed me in Pakistan when I saw a road in the mountains or in the desert that I had not yet walked or driven on. And there are also roads in life that have new experiences to transmit.

I want to have tasted all experiences: some will be unsettling and dark. How I shall cope with them, I do not yet know. To live with physical limitations in Asia is not so difficult, but certainly not easy either.

But mental limitations will be difficult for me. They will come. That I know with certainty. That challenge will perhaps be a chance to go deeper.

> I learned early in life that God never takes
> something without offering something more
> beautiful—it is up to us to find out what that is.

I learned early in life that God never takes something without offering something more beautiful—it is up to us to find out what that is. Therefore, I have tried to develop a firmly programmed yes to everything, including to the goodbye contained within and the newly opened possibility connected with it.

19

Heeding All My Calls
A Christian, a Woman, a Doctor

To Light a Candle—Victory over Frustration

I know that our work is not more than a drop of water on a hot stone. But when everyone gives one drop, his or her drop, would not the stone cool down?

I had originally tried to conduct a general practice alongside my leprosy work. Then I saw fifty patients a day. In the evening, when I came out of the office, totally exhausted, there were another fifty standing there. They cursed me because no one had examined them. The next day, I examined a hundred of them. When I left, there stood another hundred. On the third day, I realized that it was meaningless to give a hundred patients the impression that you are treating them when you are only able to make a gesture and put on a show.

There was only one possibility: to specialize the services. Then I did not have to say, "I can't treat you" and thus hurt the patient; I would say, "I am so sorry, we only have the facilities for treating leprosy patients here." Did not even our Lord, when he came into the world, restrict himself to tiny Palestine?

We are expected to tackle difficult tasks, of course, but the impossible is not expected of anyone.

The Jesuits have two mottos that I have always liked: "We do what we can, more we can't do"; and "To continue is folly, but to stop is absurd—so we'll continue."

The leprosy technicians say, "Something is better than nothing." There is also a poetic formulation for that: "It is better to light a candle than to curse the darkness." This is even better because it has a continuation: *to light a candle—and to keep it burning!*

Despite all efforts, one is always dependent on accidents, lucky events, and turns of fortune. Sometimes reality can bring one to the edge of despair. When one is on the way among the poor, you get involved not only with leprosy but also with the entire multitudes of problems: prejudices, poverty, lack of infrastructure, cultural constraints, human rights violations. You try to organize the impossible but it does not work. You try to help in local context and realize that your patient is left out. Sometimes you feel so utterly helpless, and it is just then that you decide not to give up but to try yet another route.

The Youngest of Three Brothers

His name was well known. His family was a regular donor to the cause. We had never seen them, except that one of their elegant cars would come to the MAC hospital and somebody would deliver the check. They were three brothers running a successful import/export business in Karachi.

One day, a new patient came in. He was not yet registered. He had advanced leprosy and was covered with wounds—when did we last see such a serious case? We immediately arranged admission. But where did he come from? How did we ever miss him?

The consultations continue long after night has fallen.
Photos: DAHW, Hans Kutnewsky

His history is quickly told. He was Aminuddin, the youngest of the three brothers, who in the business was responsible for the finances. One day when he and his family first suspected the disease, they took him to India. The diagnosis was established correctly. They had known since 1942 that Aminuddin had leprosy.

He kept the signs hidden over the years. Smartly tailored suits covered some of the patches. The idea of such a disease in *their* family was impossible to accept. For them, leprosy was a disease of the poor, the disgraced, those cursed by God. For this reason no doctor was ever consulted.

He was given cortisone, a drug that in long-term treatment suppresses the immunity of the patient and thus the external signs. But it worsens the disease, as it gives the bacterium, the causing agent, free rein.

As the accountant of the family enterprise, Aminuddin did not have to leave the house. He did not have to meet any of the business partners when they came to the office or when they came to the house for parties. Members of his family made Aminuddin live in concealment because of their fear of the disease and its reputation.

But then one day Aminuddin's immunity broke down completely and the disease spread with frightening speed all through his body. No longer able to nurse the patient, who was covered with wounds, at home, they finally brought him to us.

We accommodated him in a private room and did our utmost. Day and night we battled for his life—blood transfusions, antibiotics, antileprosy drugs—but we did not succeed. On the seventh day he died, with his hands in ours.

Aminuddin—he died for nothing else than *stigma*. Nothing should have prevented him from being cured, getting married, having children, and taking his rightful place in society. Stigma. Isolated at home, left alone with his suffering, inertia forced upon him. The only way to health, reporting in time to our team, was mentally blocked. When the pain got unbearable, he only increased the dose of cortisone and thus hastened his own death. This was the fate of a leprosy patient of the upper strata of society in 1985.

Who denied him his share of life and happiness? Where did *we*—all of us who make up public opinion and social beliefs—fail? True, we have always been convinced that our vocation is to serve the poor. But along the way, did we forget those few lonely ones who lead a life of hiding, in fear of being a disgrace to their families? In caring for the poor, perhaps we forgot that leprosy can also strike the rich. The question of how to reach such suffering people and how to instill confidence in those who are responsible for their health and life has been haunting me since the day when Aminuddin died through stigma in our hospital.

Twenty years later, I was just going to write that "today, it no longer happens" when Hazrat Umar from Chitral shocked us with a story.

He had registered an old lady—"fully deformed, when did I last see such a case!" She was the mother of one of our old co-workers, the clerk in the office of the district health officer; he had always been so helpful, he knew leprosy so well, we owed him a few early notifications.

And now this! "Why didn't you do anything?" I asked shocked, horrified.

"She is my mother," he said, "and when the first signs appeared, she requested that I never, ever tell anyone that she had this disease. *Never.* How could I act against her will?"

Leprosy, 2004. In Chitral. We had been working there since 1973. Whenever shall we win the battle against prejudice and fear?

Forgotten

Once, we got a visitor from Hong Kong. I cannot remember why he came. Actually, I hardly remember him at all; only faintly that he accompanied us to one of our control centers, to Malir, on the outskirts of the thirteen-million megatown, Karachi.

That morning we diagnosed a new leprosy patient, a little boy, maybe six or seven years old, a full-blown borderline leprosy patient. Sometimes, in this form of leprosy, the patient is suddenly overtaken by an acute outbreak of the disease. And so it happened to Maula Bux. Red swollen lumps all over his face, his arms, his entire body. Fever, pain all over—the boy was in acute distress. We consoled him; in six months, we said, he would laugh at the fears that haunted him now, and in two years he would be fully, totally, entirely cured. I wonder if it helped the boy at this moment of suffering, that he would be fine in two years, but it may have consoled his frightened sister who brought him for treatment.

Twelve years later our friend from Hong Kong passed through Karachi again and visited us. "For days," he said, "for weeks, Maula Bux would appear in my dreams—would that little boy whose life had not yet started, would he one day look like Zakia?"

He had, during his first stay, visited the home of our handicapped patients as well and had been confronted with Zakia, who fell victim to leprosy at the same age, around six or seven years old. Living in Afghanistan and not in Malir, the family had declared her deceased, to spare the tribe the disgrace of having a leper in its ranks. They held her captive for twenty long, *excruciating* years, hidden in a stable, until we finally rescued her on our first trip to central Afghanistan.

Zakia and Maula Bux—their stories had haunted him since he had left his visit with us.

We laughed. Maula Bux was cured, we said, and we had even taken him out of the register, which meant that he had no further problems resulting from his former leprosy!

Our friend asked, disbelievingly, if he could see him.

Well, the records were in good order. James, the leprosy technician of the area, remembered the case by name—he even still knew his house— and so he took our friend from Hong Kong along. No, Maula Bux was not at home.

Where then could they find him?

"Playing cricket," the mother said.

"Where?"

She vaguely pointed in some direction. They decided to try their luck.

In an open field, the corner littered by household rubbish, plastic bags, paper, a few banana peels, but otherwise rather clean, a team of boys was absorbed in their cricket play.

"Maula Bux," James called. A tall, handsome chap with curly hair and sparkling black eyes looked in the direction of the voice and recognized James.

"Hello."

"Keep it short," James said, "Maula Bux is busy."

"And what ... and what on earth did you feel when you were diagnosed as a leprosy patient?" our guest asked, getting straight to the point.

Maula Bux had a blank expression on his face.

"But you must remember—they made your case sheet, they gave you tablets, they explained the disease, you were sick, desperately sick at that time!"

Still no expression on Maula Bux's face to indicate any understanding.

"You were about seven!" Our visitor tried again.

James translated again.

There was a moment of silence. Maula Bux tried to recall—what did this foreigner want to know? Was there anything worth telling about his childhood? Yes, he had taken tablets, he faintly remembered, so what? He shook his head, his curly hair danced, his eyes dark as blackberries gave us a fleeting smile. "*Bhul ghaya*," he said to James, and brusquely turned to his team and after given a brief, precise command, the cricketers took position again and play resumed.

James translated: "Forgotten!"

The visitor stared for a moment at the place where Maula Bux had been standing and let out a deep sigh. He turned to James. "Thank you," he said, after a moment of reflection "or should I say 'Thank God'? Or best, thank you both!"

Women for Sale

If Rabia had not had leprosy long ago, she would not have known where to turn or whom to trust. One night she was standing at my door. After a long time she said that no, there was no problem with her disease; that was over. She came for her mother, her sister, and her two brothers.

In less than twelve hours, we were involved in a most unbelievable story. In less than twenty-four hours, we had rescued the women.

Aneela was not older than sixteen. The father, in need of money, had struck a deal with a fake *maulana* (Islamic scholar) whose business was to marry a couple prior to the "wedding" night and divorce the couple after the night, thus working around even the strict present law. Virgins fetched the best price.

The mother threw herself between the men and the victim, screaming and shrieking. The husband chained the woman, tied a cloth over her mouth and nose, and locked her inside the room. The father beat the two screaming brothers out of the house.

For security reasons, we did not dare tell anyone where we were hiding the women. It took weeks before the mother stopped mumbling and stammering "My child, my child" before she slept a night, without screaming, suddenly, "Let me go, let me go."

In this city of ten million, it took us three days to find the frightened boys, dirty and in rags, hungry and frightened.

In four months we had bought a little house in Punjab, far away from the father and his gang, where today they earn their daily living operating a small washing and ironing shop, and where they live in peace. But no charges have been brought against the husband.

Blindness—For the Sake of Honor?

There is still a blind woman who has not reported, says the compounder of the village in Lorelai District, where we have put up our emergency surgical camp.

"Blind? Both eyes?"

"Yes, both eyes."

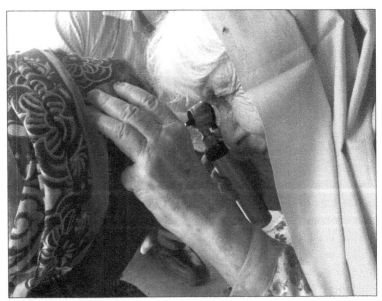

Dr. Pfau examines a patient.

We drive over to the cluster of mud huts at the slope of the bare hill. The husband allows us to examine his wife. She has cataracts and is blind, but still there is good hope that she will be able to see after the operation. We are delighted!

"Thank Allah," we say, "who has sent the surgeon right to this forgotten first aid post in your village; six months later and your wife would have been incurably blind."

"Where will you operate on her?" the husband inquires.

"In the first aid post in the village."

"I won't allow it," he says.

"We'll pick her up with the jeep and drop her off after the operation."

"I won't allow it," says the man. "A respectable woman does not leave the house of her husband. Operate on her here or you don't operate."

We leave the house after two exhausting hours of desperate efforts. Is *izzat*, tribal honor, stronger and more important than the happiness and the sight of a woman?

"*Izzat*," says Ashraf, "what kind of *izzat* is this? This is stupidity, this is sin, this is criminal!" Ashraf is active in the Tabligh movement (a strict Muslim lay group), but this, "the will of God"? Never!

We go to the village molvi. Next Friday he will give a sermon in the mosque on the duties of a husband toward his wife. The auqaf (religious affairs) minister of the province is our friend and he is from the area; he promises to make his influence felt.

We have not yet operated on the blind woman. The six months have passed.

The Dignity of Abdul Qadir

"Today …" Abdul Qadir had to take a deep breath to contain all his happiness in this small sentence. "Today I have eaten hot food. Hot food, the first time after seven years. Hot food, with my own hands! And then …" He continued the sentence with a lowered voice; he usually did not talk about it, but he had to share his relief with me. "And then I went alone to the washroom."

I had to control my tears. Abdul Qadir was able to see! Even we professionals do not fully recognize what it means for a leprosy patient to lose his eyesight. Leprosy causes hands and feet to turn numb, blunting the warning sense of pain. The disease had made it impossible for Qadir to carry out the simplest daily activities: eating, washing his face, buttoning his shirt, and going to the bathroom. Abdul Qadir could not feel a spoon and plate, he could not feel the tap or the flowing water; and at the toilet, he was fully helpless, depending on a companion to open his pajamas, lead him to the toilet, help him clean himself—all small, insignificant actions that when performed by another person cause a profound sense of loss of dignity.

And I had been so utterly helpless. Whomsoever from among my colleagues I had asked, requested, implored to operate on his cataracts, whosoever examined his eyes, had declined. There was no hope, so why take the risk?

There was no hope until Dr. Cowley, one of those kind, old-fashioned missionaries whom the world has forgotten how to produce, passed through Karachi. Dr. Cowley, for whom each person was immeasurably precious. When I shared my pain with him, he examined Abdul Qadir—thoroughly—and finally concluded that Abdul was blind. He could not make him blinder than blind but God can always perform a miracle, so let's give it a try. And God was with him and with us. After the operation Abdul Qadir could see enough to go alone to the toilet, enough to eat alone. Enough to give Abdul Qadir back his dignity.

Return to Afghanistan 2003

There was a time when we considered our Afghan refugee project a full and rousing success, when we enjoyed driving along the former slum quarters that the government had bulldozed as the refugees had been repatriated. We knew that we had played a key role in this repatriation.

And today? Oh, when we were still counting numbers, we were not aware of the rest, the dregs left over, those families who were unable to return home. These "social hardship cases" with whom we were increasingly confronted.

Indryas turns the jeep sharply into one of the narrow passages between crumbling mud houses that are as much gutter water channels as lanes. The familiar picture: torn gunny bags hung over a breech in a mud wall; barefooted children with bloated abdomens, playing in pools of gutter water, flies all over; the walls of the mud huts in precarious condition, sky shining through the roofs.

"Here," Indryas says. A boy who is peeping through a crack in the wall recognizes Indryas, rushes toward him, pulls him into the small courtyard. A brief look at his mother and he dashes out again, leaving us alone. There, on the floor, amid the mud and filth and dirt, is a young woman. Laughing, crying, uncoordinated, dirty, she can no longer control her urine and stool, a picture of utter neglect. A grenade had exploded next to her while they were fleeing from the bombing by the Americans. It hit her and she survived, but never regained her senses and is paralyzed from the hips down.

We bring her a charpoy, clean bedding, a toilet chair, a ventilator, a stove, and some crockery for the old mother who is looking after her, when she has time. The old lady is also earning the bread for the family—none of the male members of the family survived. We enter her name on our list for monthly rations.

We pass through the Afghan settlement three months later. "What happened to Balanishta?" I ask Indryas. "I'd lost track of her," he said. "The house was suddenly empty. I had been searching all over. Now I know. The entire tribe went back to Afghanistan and they took that sick woman along. They all went quietly. They had a blood feud, and if the enemy tribe had known about their departure they could have stopped them from leaving. That's why they sold everything they had and went back."

That morning, I was blissfully happy.

Forgotten and betrayed Afghanistan and her people will not give up. Clinging to their old values, they will not even forsake this sick woman, but take her all the way back home!

20

Despite Everything, the Last Word Will Be Love

The Winding Path of My Life

I am in one of the small aircrafts, a six-seater, that fly from Pakistan to Afghanistan, on a UN mission. At take-off in Islamabad, no one knew what kind of weather we were going to have. Now we are sailing like a swan on a still lake through an endless blue sky, high over a world of threatening mountains.

There were flights in which I did not know how I was supposed to hold tight to the seat and whether the plane would not in the next moment tip over and begin going down. That was on the same route, in the same plane, and with precisely the same team of pilots as this flight.

> I know from experience: life is always many-sided, colorful, contradictory, unpredictable, and never one-dimensional…. There are no answers.

And that is my life. Sometimes difficult and sometimes easy. It is a road with many turns. I know from experience: life is always many-sided, colorful, contradictory, unpredictable, and never one-dimensional. I react allergically when someone tries to put firm answers in my mouth. There are no answers. I have had phases when everything seemed to be filled with light; I have had times in which I thought how magnificent, how beautiful life is! On an external accounting, my life would indeed seem to be uncommonly successful.

But what does success really mean? And likewise, what does failure mean? When I consider the experiences of my life, I cannot sort them out into plus or minus experiences. Many failures were, in hindsight, thoroughly positive or have contained positive elements. There have been successes that later emerged as banal, that have changed nothing in my life and in the lives of other people, and have left behind no traces at all.

And then, again and again, I have had periods of depression. Is that my constitution? Is that a reaction to childhood traumas; to the war, concentration camps, and the carpet-bombing by warplanes and the ruins; to the hunger and the cold and the feeling of insecurity and unprotectedness? I do not know. Depression is certainly concentrated suffering. It is hard for me to imagine anything more burdensome. Nothing seems to make sense any longer.

Once, in the Himalayan mountains, we had successfully completed a program and came back proud and light-hearted. We had the mountain wind still in our hair. We stopped at the bazaar to buy bread for supper. A man came up to us in the jeep. He was old and careworn and offered us shoelaces to buy. Shoelaces of all things, because no one here wears laced-up shoes! His bag was still full of them and it was late afternoon.

Half an hour later we had reached our control unit. The whole team was ready to be feted. Everyone had already heard about the success of our operation. I no longer remembered the valley in which we diagnosed three early cases of children's leprosy. I no longer remembered the crystal clear sparkling mountain rivulets, the blue gentian flowers and the shiny gold of the buttercups, the butterflies and the chirping hedge sparrows. Instead I saw only the old man who wanted to sell us shoelaces.

I joined the team for a cup of tea, and I listened from afar as they told their stories of adventure. "I'm tired," I said apologetically. "You don't mind if I lie down to rest, do you?"

Why did I not buy the whole carton of laces from the man? This question will follow me still in future days.

I do not know when depression will come and when it will remain at bay. It does not permit itself to be ordered about. Once it comes, I am not even able to hope anymore that things will go differently. Nonetheless, perhaps a depressive constitution furnishes a necessary corrective against the danger of succumbing to success mentality. I should actually be happy that I have this genetic insecurity in me.

Created for Happiness

Someone once said to me that the most horrible sentence for him is this: in the end, life may turn out to be a sad invention. I maintain defiantly that the meaning of life is happiness.

The human being has a right to happiness. Happiness is natural for us. It is the final goal and the dynamic energy of life. Happiness is not apparently the fundamental structure of the world. Nonetheless, it is my experience that people are created for happiness.

> Even if I experience 99 percent unhappiness, I am
> still born for happiness. Even when I cannot tolerate
> that visceral suffering in my situation anymore and
> I would rather step out ... happiness is possible.

Even if I experience 99 percent unhappiness, I am still born for happiness. Even when I cannot tolerate that visceral suffering in my situation anymore and I would rather step out, I would still not disavow that, through it all, happiness is possible. To the contrary, I would protest and demand my right to happiness in that situation. The demand for happiness endures. If I were a political prisoner in a terror regime and facing torture, and if I then committed suicide, I would not be negating my life thereby. To the contrary, I would be asserting it in protest.

Not to continue dreaming of happiness would be as if a fish had fins but never thought to swim or a bird with wings did not intend to fly.

Despite this, there is a hope of mine that is not fulfilled in the present life of human existence. The hope is directed toward eternity. Eternity and God. These are words that, by definition, cannot be conceived with our limited understanding and with human mental categories. But if God did not really exist, how would the human being be able to invent the idea of a call that he could not even imagine? Why do I feel imprisoned in the limited nature of our ephemeral life? Why am I imprisoned in my narrow consciousness?

Even to wrestle with such questions is something outside of our biological makeup.

The place where we experience eternity is in this very life, even if we experience it here as a negative, as impassioned urge, as what is missing.

But why do we say that eternity is meant for us? Why does the human being think himself so great that he never needs real evidence to be brought forward that he really is so great? How could this concept of eternity permeate the existence of human beings so deeply if they were not created toward this higher reality?

Existentialism has applied the same argument in the reverse as evidence for the absurdity of the whole cosmos. It asks, "Why do we think that we are supposed to be immortal yet we cannot even fly?" But can an entire species have developed so perversely and nonetheless survived as a species that has developed beyond its biological environment?

That is what I, as a scientist, cannot accept. Atheism simply is not a logical possibility for me.

I have talked at length about the suffering around me and my own depression.

Kumari, twenty-eight years old. She has no hope that she will ever hold her own child in her arms or be accepted in any family. She will have to live her entire life in a home for the disabled.

Or Nasiba. We were able to extend her minimal eyesight for six years. She once believed that she was beyond danger. But now, at thirty-six years old, she is blind, has no more feeling in her hands, and has no relatives. Who will take care of her for her long life? She cannot even put a spoon to her mouth.

Not to continue dreaming of happiness would
be as if a fish had fins but never thought to swim
or a bird with wings did not intend to fly.

Or Amina, whose son joined a group of terrorists, was involved in murdering, and was caught. The boy was "such an affectionate child."

Or Mutabar, whose son landed in the drug scene. He was her only son and he had hoped he would support his parents in their advanced years.

Suffering is evil and horrible and all of life is permeated with it. How do you cope with it?

There are child beggars who devour the chicken bones, who compete for garbage that the owner of the restaurant has thrown away with the refuse onto the street.

How do you cope with that?

To perceive it, not to repress it, to have the courage to permit it to enter you, to approach you, to let it hurt you, to admit the memory of it, to stand for our uncried tears. All that is essential.

But suffering is not everything in life, and it does not have the last word. The last word will be love.

> Suffering is not everything in life, and it does not
> have the last word. The last word will be love.

I say that, despite the background of a life that, on account of my profession, stands strongly in danger of equating life with suffering. My statement is a defiant statement, a statement of hope.

Hope is never naïve. And hope entails consequences. It has the character of a summons. One must and one can *do something*. Against all facts to the contrary, hope means to wait for something intensive, even though it is not capable of being seized and held, even though it is not tangible, even though one cannot in any way be certain of getting what

Mother with an ill child waits to be treated by Dr. Pfau. Photo: DAHW, Hans Kutnewsky

one hopes for. With normal hope, a good outcome can be trusted as probable. Defiant hope does not loosen its grip and does not stop insisting on a good outcome, even against all probabilities. The external facts, the appearance to the eye, the point of departure, they are all the same in both kinds of hope.

> Defiant hope does not loosen its grip and does not stop insisting on a good outcome, even against all probabilities. The external facts, the appearance to the eye, the point of departure, they are all the same in both kinds of hope.

But what is not the same is the feeling that stands behind each of them, and the conviction in defiant hope that the sun behind the clouds *must* pierce through. And the conviction that, if the sun does not pierce through, it is nonetheless there, even when you cannot see it. When it is not carried by love and streams forth into hope, resistance cannot be kept up.

We Have the Choice

From where do I derive the courage for such hope?

Many people ask me that. I ask in reply, What else is there to do? That is the case today, no differently than forty years ago. Fundamentally the themes of our lives repeat themselves. In my case, it is the alternative that has run like a thread through my whole life: suicide or yes to life. I have decided on life.

This optimism has proven itself through to this day. I cannot negate it. Even in those moments in which I stand under a dark cloud, it has all been worth it.

We have a rule on the team, the "five-to-one rule." This rule says that when somebody or something nerves you, or you feel like raising the roof, then it is high time that you apply the five-to-one rule. Search for five good points, which in the maze of antagonizing facts you are bound to find nevertheless. The problem will fall into perspective, the situation settle, and when you now make a decision you can be sure it will be helpful and not make the whole situation worse.

The writer and philosopher Elie Wiesel once said, "You have the choice. If you decide for insanity then you can afford empathy without any boundedness. Or you can decide for remembering. Then, at minimum, you'll keep your faculties so as to pass on the memory to others."

Remembering is an active virtue against indifference. Insanity would be, in the final reckoning, a form of dropping out. Perhaps one solves the problem for oneself by dropping out. But when you attempt to remind yourselves and others of the problem, then remembering is a social service, indeed a virtue.

There are situations in which it is self-evidently clear, in both Western and Eastern culture, what is right and what is wrong. For instance, you do not leave someone alone who is in danger. You help when someone is in need. That is the case in both Afghanistan and Pakistan, just as self-evidently as it is in the West.

What we do in Pakistan is nothing extraordinarily adventuresome but rather what in every life—in the case of a single mother, in the case of a marriage—can be lived in the same way: to let yourself be moved, to help others to develop their natural tendency toward happiness, to support and not to drop out when the going gets tough. That applies in big things as well as in small things. Every individual is invited.

"A thousand people say, what can one person do?"

That is a bumper sticker that I have never forgotten.

What about investing in a counterbumper sticker: *"Tell me what a thousand people, together, cannot do!"*

Out of This Limited Condition

Perhaps the virtues of remembering are also the way to a good death. Everyone is going to die. That we will all grow old and die is the one single fact capable of being established in the world. That this fact should not play any role in my life, that I should close my eyes to it, would be for me simply too stupid. One is born and one dies. That I am going to be taken out of this limited condition—I can talk about that very openly with my team. "What are you going to do when I am no longer alive?" That sentence is not a taboo among us.

I have no regrets that life washed me up on the shores of Pakistan. There are many values in the Asian culture, which I do miss in Germany.

Dr. Pfau

In Europe, nobody would say to me as a compliment, "You are so old." Of course I am old, what is wrong with that? As if I did not have the right to be old!

The German poetess Marie Luise Kaschnitz put these words on her gravestone: "Blessed are those who lived before they died."

The art of dying that many people speak about today is connected with the art of living and with love itself.

Death is something normal. As beautiful as I find life, heaven forbid that I should have to live an additional twenty-five years.

I wish to get out of this limited condition, sometimes even quickly. I expect from death the actual fulfillment of that which I have yearned for my whole life: happiness in living and loving that goes beyond my limited condition.

And the last word will be love.

Even when my experience speaks a thousand times against it, my hope knows. It knows? Yes, it knows.

The last word will be love.

Epilogue

Without the Help of My Friends It
Would Not Have Happened

They said that we were a bunch of eccentrics, and perhaps they were right. They said that we would never succeed, as the odds were against us. But here they were wrong. Although the odds did seem against us, we made it in the end.

But really, we must have seemed a very strange crew indeed. Whenever I come across photos of the early days—Berenice, Jeannine, and me wading through the filthy water in the McLeod Road Leper Colony, that packing-case hut with the patients milling around—it looks all so unreal today, almost like some strange, surrealistic film. But it was real—very real. The thing that reinforces this reality is the amazing fact that the original team was with me for about thirty-five years.

Berenice Vargas was our pharmacist up to the 1990s. She has managed to retain some of the youth of those early days and is probably the only member of the team who can be instantly recognized in the old photos. I do not know what I would have done without her. She has helped train our leprosy technicians in pharmacy and compounding. She was responsible for our medicine, and she dispatched it to every nook and corner of Pakistan. All our patients, especially the children, have known and loved her. She has become part of their lives. Yet her role was unspectacular. Surely anyone with lesser caliber would have packed up long ago. The "little way" of Berenice Vargas, it deserves some thought. Now she has passed the eighties. Inspite of a serious illness she still participates in the life and work of MALC that she belonged to from the beginning.

It was one of "those days" in the McLeod Road Leper Colony. The patients were crowded outside and inside the hut, which was nearly bursting at the seams, when they were being examined. *Berenice* was busy in her pharmacy corner, *Abdul Rehman* and *Helen* were engrossed in their work, *Jeannine* was doing dressings and the flies were buzzing over us all. From the corner of my eye I noticed a stranger. I suppose that, in such a confined space, it would have been remarkable if I had not! But I pretended not to and went on with my examination of patients. She seemed quite out of place. Almost like a butterfly, blown off course. A very beautiful woman indeed. After a while, she announced her presence with a cough. She informed me that she was a dermatologist, that she had heard a lot about us. She then offered her services. "Oh, yes," I thought, "a familiar theme," and I continued examining patients. Quite a few begums had been to see us, their saris clutched cautiously around them as they tiptoed warily through the mire. But there was no continuity. A biryani for the patients, a few donations and no more. That evening Berenice explained that she had known the lady for some time. Her children were at the school we were running in Guru Mandir. Also she had presented a paper at a seminar on leprosy. My biggest surprise was when she returned the next day, ready for work.

She too noticed that we were a strange-looking crew, an island of foreigners. Not a single Pakistani in sight. A German doctor, a Mexican pharmacist, a Belgian nurse, an American helper, all crammed into a packing case with leprosy patients, the odor of rotting flesh and ulcers, as if it were so very, very normal.

In spite of all this, *Dr. Zarina Fazelbhoy* stayed on. She became an honorary medical officer. I feel that the program would not have taken off as well as it did if it were not for her efforts. It would have taken decades for us to make the breakthrough without her. Dr. Zarina was the first to break the concept that leprosy work was a vocation for missionaries and fools. It was only when she joined the team that outsiders began to think of the project as being *their* responsibility. Through the flair for organizing—publicity, *melas*, *tamashas*—something I had never been able to do, she was able to raise money and bring the public slowly over to our side.

Dr. Zarina was instrumental in interesting the government in the leprosy control program (I could not have endured all that bargaining). So I made the feasibility reports and she managed to convince the government. Soon after she joined the team, she began to involve her whole family in the project. I remember when she celebrated her small daughter's birthday—a party in the hospital with leprosy patients. She encouraged her boy to give tuition to the patients. The hospital's first statistics department was born on her dining room table—her children and their friends helped to compile the cards.

Above all, Dr. Zarina was able to understand that we were deadly serious. She was willing to play second fiddle in everything she did. For the sake of the leprosy patient. For the sake of the poor. Her lasting contribution is in helping the program to be seen as a Pakistani responsibility.

She left us much too early. Though she still witnessed her dream came true, that leprosy was controlled in Pakistan, we could have used her advocacy in promoting the next step, leprosy elimination, together with tuberculosis and blindness control. Dr. Zarina recovered from a serious illness and wanted to see Bombay again, the place of her birth and her studies, the place where she and her husband first met, at the university. She reached Bombay and there God called her to his heavenly kingdom, leaving the team and the patients mourning for a rare friend.

There was great need for someone to take over the administrative affairs of the MAC hospital to enable me with my co-workers to concentrate on the medical and training side. Then *the Colonel* came. He took over an administration that, in that pioneer period, had no written contracts, no rules governing annual leave, no wage agreements, and no set forms of disciplinary action. Everything had been a simple verbal agreement. He arrived in the midst of a lengthy trade union battle. Our union secretary had begun agitating for a 130 percent wage increase for all workers in the MAC hospital. Everything was coming to a standstill as a result of disruptive activities. I felt that I would not have the strength to continue. The Colonel came just in time. With a smack of strong management he set to work. With military efficiency he succeeded in smoothing out some of the problems.

His first day was memorable. He made a tour of the hospital. Then came the question, "Where exactly is my office?" I laughed, because I did not even have an office of my own. I told him that he was free to organize something for himself, and this he did. Departments were shuffled around, were combined. The result was a huge office. Into this he installed an enormous desk—at least it managed to impress visitors and applicants for work. If they had seen my tiny desk they would have wondered what *they* were going to end up with!

Another person who helped the hospital enormously was *my sister, Armgard*. She is two years older than me. At the time of her arrival the hospital was embroiled in legal problems as a result of the trade union disruption. Armgard is a law graduate. My family was rather surprised. To think that Armgard was joining *my* team! She came—and stayed seven years.

Armgard is very efficient in administrative matters and sorting out problems. She is more daring that I am and has fewer inhibitions. First, she ironed out all the legal problems. Then she set herself the enormous task of setting up a loan scheme. Loans for employees and their families. Loans for the destitute. She has a gift for writing. Her tour reports were so vivid, her analysis of situations so clear, that the reader felt that he was actually accompanying her. She has a sense of humor, a necessary requirement for anyone wanting to survive and keep sane in this field of leprosy work.

She used to do all things I had always wanted to do—helping individuals in a mess, unravelling it all and setting them on their feet again. This is one of the things I want to do when I reach semiretirement age, when I have more time. I am a member of a religious order and have a lifelong commitment, therefore I have no problems regarding security for the future. Armgard had a family in Germany. She wanted to see her new granddaughter; she was rightly concerned about her pension. The longer one is away, the less one eventually gets. These reasons forced her to return, but our seven years together were happy and unforgettable.

Safia Khan came to us through Dr. Zarina. They had known each other at school in Poona and the friendship had continued when they came to Pakistan after 1947.

She was an educationalist. Her last assignment was as headmistress of the Karachi New Town Government Girls School. The new school is now named after her. She wanted to do something after retirement—to serve humanity—and Dr. Zarina brought her to us. She worked in an honorary capacity for the Marie Adelaide Leprosy Center. Inspired by the slogan "It is better to light a candle than to curse the darkness," she visited schools all over Pakistan, taught the facts about leprosy, showed slides, inaugurated a matchbox competition, and raised enormous sums of money.

She taught English to the trainees in the leprosy technicians course. The students from far-flung areas, whose educational standards were poorer than the others, remember her keen interest and infinite patience.

A modest, simple lady, she came to work by bus. Even when very ill, she covered up her final illness bravely. When we inquired about her health, she would say, with that typical merry twinkle in her eyes, "It is only a touch of gripe."

Miss Safia Khan was a woman on the side of freedom. A champion for the underdog. A campaigner for basic rights. Perhaps it was significant that she died on Pakistan Day. Although Safia Khan was not with us from the very beginning, she was one who stuck it out. She stayed on—until the very end.

And today?

Recently I woke up in the intensive care unit in Karachi. My first thought, "How good—thank you—the program is in safe hands." This is really a gift from heaven for me. The work will continue in the spirit in which we started it. We have worked at it long enough. When we still were in the wooden shed in the leper colony, Jeannine and Berenice and I, we had already agreed on one objective: really successfully, we stated, we shall have our mission only completed when we are no longer missed.

It turned out to take longer, and it was more complicated than we had anticipated. When I celebrated my thirty-fifth birthday, an unforgettable celebration with thirty-five red roses (in Karachi!), I swore to myself that my successor will be in charge when he is thirty-five years old, too—the age was just too wonderful to be missed! I hit this deadline. *Dr. O. M.* has been with us for twenty-one years, first as my crown prince, then as the ruling authority. He is honest, hardworking, professionally and exceptionally capable, so he climbed the ladder a bit too fast. When he reached the top, there was nowhere else to climb to. So we tried it with the WHO; he worked (still for the program) with the Worldbank, international organizations, which paid their expert salaries, and we developed different priorities. Misunderstandings deepened and in a long, painful process, we had to separate. We belonged to two worlds, which will never be able to meet. We can work together, but we cannot share and live together.

Today, we know it was the right decision. Dr. O. M. is happy in a job that takes him out of the nitty-gritty, time- and energy-consuming work at the operational level, where we in MALC derive our happiness and satisfaction.

As for the present management group, we have a long, long story, a life story together. *Dr. Ashfaq* joined as a young graduate. During the Indo-Pakistan war in 1971, he went to the army and returned as soon as he got a chance: "The challenge the leprosy work offers, this challenge you do not find anywhere else!" Today he is chief executive officer (CEO), not only of MALC but of the entire NGO component of the National Leprosy Control Program, and deputy federal advisor to the government of Pakistan. He is a born team leader. His most precious contribution—his inborn communication skills; the rest you can learn, slowly learn, but it is possible to learn it. But goodwill toward others, you better bring that along in a management position! Dr. Ashfaq relies heavily on his management team, the executive council (EC): the chief executive officer, the medical director, the administrative director, the finance director—quite a team!

Dr. Zia, the medical director, the reliable and loyal doctor with his sense for exact diagnosis, could also have taken up the writing profession, I think. The book he wrote, *Serving the Unserved*, is slowly developing into a hit. Written in English, it will soon have a Sindhi translation. And the leading English newspaper is always happy to print his contributions. On the team, we appreciate his ability to put facts convincingly together—in most of the publications that leave MALC you can discover Dr. Zia's handwriting. And his instinctive unfailing right moral judgment—I have often been delighted to witness his interventions.

Premachandra from Sri Lanka, the finance director, has a strong social conscience, a simple lifestyle, a heart for people in distress. He simultaneously amazes me again and again with his shrewd professional knowledge, with which he is operating the financial affairs of the organization! It was he who introduced the welfare activities operated and "owned" by the staff, which turned into a sound and clean financial enterprise. No, adherence to rules is not his cup of tea. Be prepared that he will work if not twenty-fours then at least eighteen hours a day, and then he will lump all the accumulated time together and disappear in the direction of Sri Lanka. And when Mr. Prem disappears to Sri Lanka, you only can pray that he will return in the foreseeable future and you will never be sure when. But return he will, like all those on the team who have been infected not with the leprosy bacillus (leprosy is curable today) but with the leprosy work bacillus—and then you are incurably ill!

Mervyn Lobo,—I stole him from Dr. O. M.—was the youngest and doubtlessly brightest on the team, at that time not yet in the top management. Eight years we have shared our common work and concerns in the provinces, our problems and successes. We have braved suicidal bus and jeep trips; landslides in the Kashmir mountains, Lobo's hands firmly grasped around mine while we struggled to escape the mudslide as we hardly managed to pull our feet out of the sticky mess (and save the luggage in addition). We have enjoyed the breathtaking beauty of the country and mused over the strange mentality of the mountain tribes. How deeply these years knitted us together, I only realized after we returned to Karachi and Lobo took over as director of administration and the adventures were over (regretfully). Or rather they changed their nature. Now the challenge was to manage a National Leprosy-TB-Blindness Control Program.

When MALC, in the early nineties, recovered from the administrative chaos it had slumped into, it was due to his efficiency. When MALC has a problem, as now the need to establish the fundraising department and step up the resource development, the team will call on Lobo. When one of the staff members gets caught in a police raid, it will be Lobo who, together with Zahoor, gets the man out of the police station and saves him from torture. I would not know what MALC would do without Lobo's input.

The EC, it is really a group, and an interfaith team, too! Dr. Ashfaq, a committed Muslim, a Sunni; Mr. Prem, a Buddhist, a typical Buddhist, anyone could diagnose him as a Buddhist; Dr. Zia, a rather new Catholic; and Mr. Lobo, a born Catholic—all knitted together as a group with the same mission.

There are others without whom I never would have made it: *Mohammed Ashraf,* eighteen years in the mountains as leprosy technician, then responsible for the Leprosy-Tuberculosis Control Program in Azad Kashmir; *Mohammed Ali,* the youngest of the leprosy field officers, responsible for leprosy and tuberculosis control in the Northern Areas, from Gilgit to Skardu; *Hamid Shah,* who controlled leprosy in the vast desert areas of Balochistan and has been a friend to me all along; *Syed Azadar Houssain*, who motivated his team to achieve the same in Sindh; *Abdul Hamid* who did it in the jungle of Karachi, tackling successfully the impossible task to control leprosy in a town of thirteen million inhabitants; *Qurban*, who braved all hardships in central Afghanistan for sixteen long years, until the Taliban occupation forced him to save his wife and children and flee to Pakistan. How often have we staked our lives in the efforts to reach outpatients, celebrated our narrow escape, planned for new challenges and new adventures!

And the middle management, the group who is reorganizing the training department with and for me: *Ilyas*, my PA in Islamabad; *Francis*, the last resort when nobody knows what to do next, and he finds the missing paper or the right contact address who will then come to our help; the Interprovincial Coordination Department with whom I can discuss any and everything, and who will implement it, from human rights interventions to the logistics of antituberculosis drug provision, changes in government promotional rules, statistical evaluations, the repair of the jeeps, and a new e-mail connection; the district leprosy controllers, who ensure that the government health services deliver leprosy, tuberculosis, blindness control services to thousands of needy patients.

That is 480 co-workers in Pakistan, and everyone has his or her contribution, from the top management to the drivers. Everyone is unique. Conflicts are faced squarely, and in a violence-ridden society, ways of nonviolent conflict solutions explored. So they will be prepared to face the challenges of the future.

Looking Back Over Forty Years

Who are we? I ask one of our co-workers. A pensive moment. Then Mervyn smiles. "We," he says, "are a group of ordinary people who decided to do the extraordinary—and succeeded in it."

That is right. The extraordinary. Over 50,300 leprosy patients identified in this country of 140 million inhabitants, in mountain caves and tents in the desert, in the endless congested slum quarters in the big cities, with a cure rate of 97 percent. Hundreds of thousands of friends gained, friends from and for the forgotten, the marginalized, the voice for the silent sufferers.

In 1960 we started in a wooden shed in the leper ghetto on McLeod Road, near Karachi's bank quarter, ridiculed by colleagues, suspiciously watched by patients, with exactly twenty rupees in our pockets. Within three years we had established a modern hospital in the center of Karachi. In eight years we had convinced the government to embark with us on a countrywide leprosy control program. In 1980 the hospital was recognized as a national training institute. In 1996 we had controlled leprosy in Pakistan.

Looking back over those forty years, I am happy. Happy in spite of all the misery we went through in Pakistan, in Afghanistan. Happy in spite of all organizational and financial problems, which at present seem pretty much insurmountable, but we shall find a way.

Dr. Pfau in 2014.

Who will continue? Leprosy is controlled but not eradicated. It cannot be eradicated, probably never, with an incubation period of two to five to even forty years, with eight hundred to a thousand new cases annually in Pakistan, with seven hundred thousand worldwide. It is not only the question of conquering the leprosy bacillus, the causing agent of the disease. This we can do with a triple drug combination; it will not be too difficult. But what about all the long-term damage caused by the disease: broken relationships; disappointed friendships; lost opportunities; deformed hands, feet, faces; dim eyesight; plans that never come to fruition? Who can list the suffering the disease has caused and is still causing, though we have controlled leprosy and the World Health Organization (WHO) has deleted Pakistan from the list of leprosy affected countries. "Plain lie," the leprosy technicians say, and they know what they are talking about. *Leprosy* finished? The *disease* overcome? Never! We just have controlled the leprosy *germ*, not more.

Eighteen thousand patients are awaiting effective disability services in Karachi alone. Twenty-three thousand patients and their families have to be accompanied through the process of rehabilitation, to regain their dignity, their self-esteem; children have to be admitted in schools; and the community—140 million people in Pakistan—won over to accept them in society.

No, *cure* has only been achieved when our patients finally have access to the seven human rights we are claiming in Pakistan, too: the right to food, clothing, and shelter; access to basic health services and primary education; social acceptance; and equal chances in the labor market (whatever this may mean in the local context). Only when all this is again accessible to them do we declare them *cured*. An uphill task.

It is not easy to convince the government to continue with our entire infrastructure, even though the caseload has decreased dramatically. The workers, too, are no longer satisfied: when after a long walk through the mountains, you finally reach one cluster of mud houses, and you examine everyone and declare, thank Allah, you have no leprosy, there are still old people in danger of going blind, emaciated babies, coughing mothers.

We therefore started work, together with leprosy, on tuberculosis and blindness control. This gives the staff the feeling of being needed and appreciated again. In tuberculosis we can save lives, often most dramatically. We have already cured over one hundred thousand patients. In blindness control, we often can restore eyesight, every time a moment of utter happiness. We treated 233,116 eye patients alone in 2002.

This is our dream, that this successful leprosy program, with the infrastructure established, will extend their services to a large number of general patients as well: tuberculosis patients, eye patients. And that services are established that are person-centered, keeping the preciousness of each individual patient in mind.

"I was so upset," says Mohammed Ali, returning from one of his field trips. "I was positively mad. There they knew that the little girl has a spinal TB; of course they know that she is in pain, that she will be seriously deformed before she has grown up, so that her first delivery will endanger her life if she has no access to caesarean operation. I just could not remain quiet. 'Are you a Mussulman?' I asked the doctor. 'You know you have to answer on the last day of judgment; what will you say if the girl has died?' He looked somewhat puzzled. And worried. And now, I am so happy, now the WHO treats all extra pulmonary patients, too!"

This is the future. We are one of the few, if not the only group who has decades-long experience in handling communities. We are a group with a strong "c. i.," with a corporate identity, keeping its values intact. Thanks to God that the group is continuing its prophetic role, while rendering professionally sound and humanly warm services to *leprosy*, *tuberculosis* and *eye patients*.

And this will not be the last—already, AIDS is at our door.

If you want to help us to reach those who have no other succor …

Chronological Table

Events of Personal Significance	Events of Historical Significance	
1929 Ruth Pfau is born in Leipzig, Germany		
	1939	World War II begins
	1945	May 8, World War II ends in Europe; Germany divides into western and eastern parts August 6 and 9, atomic bombs explode above the Japanese cities of Hiroshima and Nagasaki; World War II ends in Asia; on these two days 130,000 civilians are killed, 100,000 seriously wounded
	1946	Nuremberg war-crimes trials are conducted
1947 Graduates from high school	1947	British rule in India ends; Pakistan as a nation state is created
	1947– 1948	Berlin airlift conducted by western Allies
	1948	State of Israel is founded

Events of Personal Significance	Events of Historical Significance	
	1948	Kashmir dispute leads to border tension between India and Pakistan; currency reform in western Germany leads to "Economic Miracle" of German reconstruction during next two decades
	1949	Federal Republic of Germany (west) and the German Democratic Republic (east) are founded
	1949–1950	Mao Tse-tung is victorious in the Chinese Civil War; China becomes communist
1950 Begins medical education in Mainz. 1953 changes to Marburg.	1950	The Korean War begins
1951 Baptized in Protestant Students' Parish at the University of Mainz in the Lutheran faith		
1953 Received in the Catholic Church	1953	Workers revolt in East Berlin suppressed by USSR tanks
	1954	Fortress of Dien Bien Phu falls; end of the French power in Vietnam

Events of Personal Significance	Events of Historical Significance
1956 Receives medical degree	
1956 Interns in medical hospital in Winterberg in the region of Sauerland	
1957 Receives medical doctorate	
1957 Enters the noviciate of the Order of the Daughters of the Heart of Mary	
1958 Studies internal medicine in Cologne	
1959 Studies gynecology and obstetrics in Bonn	
1960 Emigrates to Karachi, Pakistan. Starts leprosy work in the leprosy ghetto in Karachi, in Marie Adelaide Dispensary	
1961 Dr. Zarina Fazelbhoy joins the project	1961 Berlin Wall is erected
1963 Marie Adelaide Leprosy Dispensary, the hut in the leper colony, is shifted onto hospital premises in the center of Karachi and becomes Marie Adelaide Leprosy Center (MALC)	1962 The Cuban Missile Crisis

Events of Personal Significance	Events of Historical Significance
	1963 America begins engagement in Vietnam
1965 Starts training programs for leprosy assistants	1965 India-Pakistan War
	1968 Student revolt in the capitals of Western Europe and the United States
1969 (May) Receives medals: the Cross of Merits of the Federal Republic of Germany and the Sitara-i-Quaid-e-Azam medal in Pakistan	
1971 Recognition of MALC as National Training Institute for Leprosy	1971 War in East Pakistan; state of Bangladesh is created
1975 Start of tuberculosis control program in Azad Kashmir, and of blindness control program in Balochistan.	1975 Vietnam War ends
	1977 General Zia-ul-Haq stages a nonviolent military coup and becomes Pakistan's president

Events of Personal Significance	Events of Historical Significance	
1978 (Aug.)	Receives Great Cross of Merits of the Federal Republic of Germany; also the highest civilian Pakistani honor: the Half Moon		
		1979	Soviet invades Afghanistan
1980	Becomes national advisor for leprosy for Pakistan by the Pakistani government for Azad Kashmir and TB control program		
1981	Constitution of the National Leprosy Control Board		
1984	Goes illegally into Afghanistan		
1984	Begins building a leprosy control program in Afghanistan		
1985	May 5, twenty-fifth anniversary of medical service in Pakistan; receives the Great Cross of Merits with Stars of the Federal Republic of Germany	1985	Mikhail Gorbachev becomes general secretary of Soviet Communist Party and president of the USSR

Events of Personal Significance	Events of Historical Significance
1986 Begins building on a leprosy assistance program in Afghanistan	
	1987 Soviet troops pull out of Afghanistan
	1989 First large-scale incident of ethnic violence in Sindh
	1989 Berlin Wall toppled by East German protest movement
	1990 Germany reunifies into one country
	1991 Soviet Empire ends; most of the former Soviet Republics become independent
	1994 Taliban emerges as rival group to the warring mujahideen faction
	1995 Ethnic riots in Karachi escalate into civil war
1996 Leprosy control achieved; hands over program to the Pakistani management team	1996 On New Year's Day, MQM snipers kill fourteen people, including five law enforcers and five members of a family
Leprosy is controlled in Pakistan, prevalence below one case in ten thousand population	1996 Taliban captures Kabul and impose Islamic system of government

Events of Personal Significance	Events of Historical Significance	
1975 1981	Start of TB control program in Azad Kashmir In Northern Areas, Pakistan, national start of blindness control program in Balochistan, North-West Frontier Province, Sindh		
		1999 (Oct.)	General Musharaf takes over
1999– 2002	Constitution of National Leprosy Tuberculosis Blindness Control Board; the "Triple Merger Strategy" (leprosy, TB, blindness) is officially notified by the government	2001	On September 11, Al-Qaeda attacks the Pentagon in Washington, DC, and destroys the World Trade Center in New York City; about four thousand people die; United States invades Afghanistan
2003	Implementation of the "Triple Merger Strategy" across Pakistan	2003	U.S. troops invade Iraq
2004 (July)	MALC is present in the Internet: www.malc.org.pk		

About the Publisher

The Crossroad Publishing Company publishes Crossroad and Herder & Herder books. We offer a 200-year global family tradition of books on spiritual living and religious thought. We promote reading as a time-tested discipline for focus and understanding. We help authors shape, clarify, write, and effectively promote their ideas. We select, edit, and distribute books. With our expertise and passion we provide wholesome spiritual nourishment for heart, mind, and soul through the written word.